FEARLESS PARENTING

FOR THE NEW MILLENNIUM

PROTECT YOUR CHILDREN FROM WHAT PARENTS FEAR THE MOST: TERRORISM, SCHOOL VIOLENCE, SEXUAL EXPLOITATION, ABDUCTION AND KIDNAPPING

By

Dr. Helen Boehm

ISBN: 1-4140-4475-5 (e-book)
ISBN: 1-4140-4474-7 (Paperback)

Library of Congress Control Number: 2003099050

This book is printed on acid free paper.

Printed in the United States of America
Bloomington, IN

1stBooks - rev. 02/07/04

This book is dedicated to Ernie Allen, John Rabun and the staff and Board of Directors of the **National Center for Missing and Exploited Children**. The National Center's unwavering commitment to protecting and educating America's families and has given all of our children a powerful voice in courtrooms and in Congress.

The National Center's founding parents are Reve' and John Walsh, whose 6-year-old son, Adam, was abducted and murdered in 1981. Over the last two decades, they have advocated on behalf of child safety and championed victim's rights throughout the country. Along with John's relentless pursuit of predators who victimize children on his TV show, *"America's Most Wanted*," the Walshs' commitment and example continue to inspire me.

National Center Board members, Patty Wetterling; mother of Jacob, missing since 1989 and Colleen Nick; mother of Morgan, missing since 1995, have also turned their personal heartbreak into national legislative and child-protection initiatives. Their courage and resolve have earned my admiration and respect.

Finally, to all parents who must get up each morning and live each day knowing the answer to the question, "What if?" I commemorate the legacy and significance of your children's lives with this book.

Helen Boehm

CONTENTS

It has been said that if you live at the ocean's edge, you can either build a fence around your house - - - or, you can teach your kids how to swim. We can't isolate our children or prevent them from participating in the challenges of life. Instead, we must teach them to survive and to thrive in a world filled with danger and risk.

We must teach them how to swim.

WHAT IF…?

The flight attendant holds an oxygen mask high above her head for all passengers to see. She then explains that if the aircraft's cabin should lose pressure during flight, the masks will automatically drop down in front of each seat. And then she repeats a familiar warning to those passengers who are traveling with young children: "Secure the oxygen mask over your own nose first, *before* securing the mask of your child".

Parents, today, face risks that our parents' generation could never even have imagined. Troubling new threats—including bio-terrorism, school shootings and sexual assaults—require fresh approaches and innovative solutions. These are particularly turbulent times and parents must be knowledgeable and confident about protecting themselves *before* they can begin to safeguard their children! Surely, none of us should miss the opportunity to keep our children safe because of a lack of information or preparation to do so. We can no longer sit back and *hope* the "pressure in the cabin" will never drop!

Parenting smarter - and safer - in this new millennium will require that everyone who cares for and about children understand the risks facing today's families and know what to do about them. In order to "childproof" and protect vulnerable youngsters, parents must be able to act quickly and correctly; put *their* oxygen masks on, *first,* and then guide their kids to safety.

If children are our nation's passion, their security is, truly, our national obsession. Since the tragic events of September 11, 2001, America's family priorities have intensified and a deep national preoccupation with the safety of our children has emerged. But, many parents are simply overwhelmed with fear and believe that danger in the world is out of control—and, out of *their* control. They want to be proactive about protecting their families—but they simply don't know how.

Parents worry about many things. They're scared about what might happen to their kids on the way to school, in the mall or in a car. They're concerned about the newly released criminal in the next town, the man next door, the babysitter they have just hired and the minister they have known for years. They're anxious because they would like to keep their families secure, but can't guarantee that their children are protected from crime and violence - even in their own homes.

A steady focus on prevention, information and preparation <u>can</u> provide confidence and assurance while fostering family resilience. As parents learn new strategies for keeping children safe, they will develop the strength and resolve necessary to lead their families by their own example. Behaviors that adults use to shield and protect *themselves* will surely be noticed and modeled by their children.

Of course, there are no guarantees that any amount of information or readiness can provide perfect control or total safety for your family. Children will experience some risk in their daily interactions as an unavoidable fact of life. Even the most vigilant, caring and safety-oriented parents cannot *totally* eliminate their children's vulnerability. But, parents can minimize the risks that their children face by anticipating and reducing situations that could, potentially, put them in harm's way. Even though one cannot remove every sharp edge or potential risk from the environment, parents can recognize and predict dangers to their families and respond, appropriately, to them. By managing some threats and treating others, parents can diminish the risks faced by their children and empower their kids to do the same. It is not more difficult to *become* a parent in this post-Columbine era, but it is, certainly, far more challenging to *be* one!

As a "parenting expert" for Disney's Internet website, family.com, I had the opportunity to speak with parents across the country regarding their deepest concerns and most closely held fears concerning children's safety. With the gracious assistance of researchers at the Institute for Mental Health Initiatives (IMHI) of the George Washington University School of Public Health in Washington, DC, I was able to expand these conversations to determine specific areas of risk that required additional parent education and support. This book, therefore, responds to the most significant worries of parents today. This is not a statistical analysis of the most lethal possibilities that children face but, rather, practical information and guidance about the dangers that parents, themselves, fear the most.

By minimizing children's vulnerability to **terrorism, school violence, and abduction, kidnapping and exploitation**—the contemporary dangers that parents fear most—it is my hope that families will feel empowered to be proactive and effective in safeguarding their children. So, put on your oxygen masks. Although the statistical risks, as you will read, are very low…the stakes - *the well being of all of our children* - are very high.

PART I

TERRORISM

WHAT IF...
MY CHILD IS A VICTIM OF TERRORISM?

The security and safety of family life in America was permanently shattered by the shocking terrorist attacks of September 11, 2001. Since that horrific day, the continuing threat of terrorism has brought a renewed appreciation of life and family as well as a heightened sensitivity to the awesome responsibilities of parenting in this new millennium. Today, families continue a safeguarding vigil, as the realities of war, terrorism and threats of destruction throughout the world inundate the news and permeate our everyday lives. Now, we must know what to do "if"...Parent smarter, learn more and *do* more to keep our children safe. Homeland security begins at home.

Terrorist bombings, biological attacks, hijackings or any aggressive strike that targets innocent people, particularly children, for harm is truly incomprehensible to either understand or accept. Nothing can ever prepare a parent for the horror of this type of action. Although such a hideous disregard for human life is unbearable to even fathom, parents must live with the potential risk of increasing acts of terrorism on United States' soil, as well as throughout the world.

According to First Lady Laura Bush, "On September 11th, America faced terrorist attacks of the worst kind. Innocent lives were lost and a sad cloud was cast over this great nation. These acts were intended to cause fear among all Americans - including our children. But, we *cannot* let that happen. There are things that we can do to help our kids. Talk with them, listen to them. Tell them they're safe, and that they're loved."

Parents want and need to do everything in their power to safeguard and protect their children. When asked, "Can we prepare our families to deal with terrorism?" I can only answer, "In this new millennium—how can we *not*?"

There is no "Parenting 101" textbook, complete with a chapter on how to safeguard your family during a terrorist attack or road map for safe passage when this type of unpredictable disaster strikes. But, thoughtful planning and considered responses based on the most complete information available will provide some of the comfort and confidence that families will need to deal with terrorism. Although no one expects horrible events to occur, they can and, unfortunately, they do. Therefore, parents must prepare their children for potentially painful and challenging situations present in the increasingly complex—and often dangerous world in which we now live. Luckily, children are strong, resilient and able to endure even under the most challenging circumstances.

WHEN TERROR STRIKES: FIRST THINGS FIRST

Although the following will sound simple, it is not simplistic: When terror strikes, parents must take care of themselves first…and *then* take care of their children.

Your children depend on you, completely, and model their actions and behaviors after yours. Your example will be invaluable and your strength, calm and resolve will be critical in establishing a pattern for children's emotional adjustment and behavior. As an adult, you'll need to manage your own fears prior to dealing with the anxieties of your children. Children who perceive adults to be powerless exhibit increased anxiety. Psychologist Eric Erikson reflected that young children who had little or no confidence in the power of adults to control situations would likely come to doubt all adult authority as they grew up and act out with anti-social behavior.

During a crisis, it is necessary for parents to act in ways that will communicate confidence and authority. And, it is also the responsibility of parents to help diminish the anxieties and nervous energy of their children. Mothers and fathers are considered "first responders" in a terrorist attack and must be emotionally available to reassure children, from the first news of such an event, that they - and many others—will be there to protect them and do everything possible to keep kids safe.

The enormity and uncertainty of terrorism demands that parents demonstrate to their families - in both words and actions - that they are strong and will work hard to keep day-to-day existence as secure and stable as possible. Although life rarely comes with 100% guarantees of safety, a crisis situation accentuates the need for children to feel as secure and unthreatened as possible at home, in school and in their immediate communities. Children need to feel that their surroundings are safe and that the adults in their lives will maintain a sense of control and authority.

Although young children are extraordinarily resilient, research shows that their strength and flexibility is predicated on an attachment to a parent or other significant adult. This attachment and trusting bond is the foundation for life-long emotional development and stability. Under traumatic circumstances, this relationship is particularly necessary—but also, can be volatile. Stress occurs when a parent is either emotionally or physically "unavailable" or when a child feels that a separation from a parent is imminent.

With all due respect to our highest government officials and religious leaders, in the eyes of the young child, it is *parents* who have nothing less than the wisdom of Solomon and the courage of David against Goliath. Parents are the CEO's of their families, the Rock of Gibraltar and able to leap tall buildings!

During a crisis, the role of parent will be the most challenging part that any mother or father has ever played. Perhaps, our entire experience of parenting, nurturing and protecting youngsters has been a rehearsal for just such an event. Without being able to influence governments, world leaders or terrorist organizations, your unconditional love for your children will, ultimately, be the most powerful force in preserving the safety and well being of your family.

CHILDREN'S REACTIONS TO TERRORISM

Terrorism is a traumatic event. "Trauma" refers to a serious bodily injury, painful wound, or shock. The term is used by emergency room physicians to describe patients requiring immediate emergency medical intervention as well as by psychologists to explain severe distress and emotional anguish. Trauma can include psychological suffering, require immediate professional attention and be long lasting.

A child's individual reaction to trauma, and how that behavior is handled and responded *to*, will determine each child's readiness to move from the status of trauma "victim" to trauma "survivor". Parents are, of course, a critical part of this process and can greatly influence their children's "victim" or "survivor" perceptions.

Children worry about terrible things that might occur. But, when terrorism strikes, something horrible *has* occurred. Be aware that after a disaster, young children are most afraid for their own safety and also that:

- They will be separated from family and left alone
- The event will happen again
- Someone they love will be injured or killed

Whether a child has experienced terrorism first hand or has been exposed—even inadvertently - to news coverage or adult conversation about a massive crisis situation—an extreme sense of vulnerability can occur. And, an event of major proportion may even reinforce the magical thinking of youngsters; *if I imagined it and it was my idea...did I cause it to happen?*

Children's individual reactions to terrorism can vary greatly and are determined by many factors including, the nature of their connection to the event, their immediate environment, family response, resiliency, maturity, previous experiences, temperament and personality. Although each child is unique, there are similarities in the reactions and needs of youngsters as they are influenced by thoughts of terrorism. In response to the news of a terrorist attack, therefore, parents may expect to see their children exhibit some of the following behaviors:

- "Acting out" and other discipline problems at home and in school
- Physical complaints including nausea, headache and weight changes
- Distractibility and the inability to concentrate on simple tasks
- Sadness, decreased physical activity and social withdrawal
- Bedtime and sleep disturbances, nightmares and increased fearfulness
- Anxiety, nervousness and a preoccupation with the traumatic event
- Fear for the safety of parents, grandparents, relatives and friends
- Dread of travel, separation from parents, leaving home or being alone
- Acute agitation, pacing and angry verbal outbursts
- Regressive behaviors such as bedwetting and thumb sucking
- Fear of going to school (School Phobia)
- Exaggerated new anxieties—fear of monsters, burglars and "bad guys"

- Severe tantrums, laughing or crying spells
- Depression and a sense of hopelessness about life and the future
- Dangerous, risk-taking and attention-getting behaviors
- Obsessive thinking about possible dangers to parents or to themselves
- Excessive expectation and thinking that another terrorist event will occur
- Feelings of vulnerability, powerlessness and helplessness
- Obsessive, repeated thoughts like a "video loop" about the traumatic event that "intrude" while involved in another thought or activity

THE EMOTIONAL IMPACT OF TERRORISM ON CHILDREN

After an event as horrifying as a terrorist attack, children may suffer psychological and emotional stress that is as acute, limiting and serious as any physical injury. In the first days and weeks following the traumatic event it will be important for parents to closely monitor the reactions and behaviors of their children and maintain a constant foundation of support, comfort and acceptance. Parents should be pro-active about creating opportunities for interaction, discussion and a sharing of feelings. When the lines of communication and trust are flowing, potential problems can be averted and a child's anxiety can be minimized before becoming serious or even overwhelming.

Parental acceptance of the wide range and variety of ways children react to adversity is crucial to fully restoring normal family life. Some children will be consumed by obsessive worry, waiting for another attack to occur, while others may have no immediate reaction to a terrorist strike at all. Still others will be plagued with shame and guilt believing they were partially responsible for the terrible events or for not preventing them in some way. Although these reactions may be illogical, children's concerns must be listened to, recognized and treated with serious regard.

Behavioral reactions to traumatic events can be intense but also, delayed or even denied. Youngsters, therefore, can be reassured with both firmness and love that life *will* improve and *will* return to normal. Optimistic assurances will help children feel safe and will enable them to develop a more positive outlook on the future. Self-awareness and an opportunity to share feelings will enable the healing process to begin.

Depression: Children - as well as adults—can become depressed. Depression is usually described as a strong feeling of sadness and hopelessness that persists and interferes with one's ability to fully function. During periods of stress, children are at particular risk for depression. Therefore, following a terrorist event, parents should be alert for one or more of the following behaviors that might signal their youngster's depression:

- Feelings of sadness and sorrow
- Lack of joy in previously enjoyed activities
- Acting out and attention-getting behaviors
- Expressions devoid of enthusiasm or hope
- Lack of excitement in joyful things and increased boredom
- Using phrases like, "I wish I was dead" or "You would be better off if I wasn't alive"

- Hyper-sensitivity to criticism and failure
- Shyness, isolation and retreat from others
- Increased anger and aggressive behavior
- Severe change in sleep patterns and energy cycles
- Increased headaches, nausea and stomach-aches

Early diagnosis, psychological counseling and medical intervention each play an important role in the successful treatment of depression in children. New medical strategies, including play therapy and recently introduced medications have shown beneficial effects. Like many of today's most troubling ailments, depression in children requires professional assistance and a comprehensive treatment plan.

Anxiety: All children have fears and a normal amount of trepidation about scary things like the dark, parents leaving, monsters, getting lost, strangers, etc. Although some anxiety is necessary and important in maintaining general alertness, extreme anxiety can be paralyzing in its effects. When emergencies or disasters interrupt a child's dependable routine, debilitating anxiety and excessive nervous behaviors may appear.

Following a terrorist attack, anxiety and constant worry should be carefully monitored. Parents should watch for changes in demeanor including any of the following behaviors:

- Pervasive and non-specific feelings of nervousness and worry
- Constant thoughts about something bad happening
- Distractible behaviors

- Repetitive thoughts about the terrorist event and additional possible attacks in the future
- Inability to concentrate
- Separation anxiety
- Phobias and new situations to be feared or avoided
- Constant need for assurance of safety from parents and teachers
- Concern about "going first" or trying new things
- Suspicion of new people and places
- Increased physical complaints including racing heart
- Nightmares
- Extreme fear of leaving home, sleepovers or something bad happening to parents when the child is not at home to protect or save them

A therapeutic approach comprised of counseling, play therapy and, in some cases, medication can provide youngsters with strategies to manage anxious situations. This type of comprehensive treatment, particularly when initiated at the first signs of excessive anxiety, can help to prevent the development of full-blown phobias or fears of activities like school, swimming, elevators and airplanes.

REACTIONS TO TERRORISM AT DIFFERENT AGES

Preschool Children: For preschoolers, classroom routines—from rest to snack to clean-up-time—provide structure, consistency and reassurance. Predictable behavior patterns and routines help young children feel secure and in control. In the case of a terrorist attack, a lack of routine and predictability can render a preschooler fearful and insecure. Any disruption in stability can cause anxiety that is compounded by constant worry about abandonment and separation.

The love and consistency of parents can strongly affect the preschooler's emotional stability. Preschool children will cling to parents and teachers and will often be consumed with worry about their parents during the school day. Many preschoolers will not understand the permanency of death, so their constant questions reflect their expectation that terrorism—and any deaths that may be associated—can be reversed.

Behavior such as changes in play and items in children's drawings may reveal a continuing preoccupation with the terrorist event and a prolonged interest in the details of what has happened. These scenarios help to organize and communicate concerns and may likely include reenactments of abandonment and family separations.

Fearful reactions, however, are not always reflected in behavior or play. Parents must be mindful of children's ability to suppress or avoid revealing their worries and keeping all of their concerns tucked deeply within. These children, in particular, may need the closeness and safety of a one-to-one situation with a parent or trusted adult, to fully understand and describe their worries, even when they have not demonstrated any outward reactions to the traumatic event.

***Helping Preschool Children Cope With Their Fears*:** Young children need parents' firm assurances that caring adults will keep them safe and secure. It should be a heartfelt promise delivered with confidence and certainty.

Existing routines should be observed and new schedules established. Familiar routines will bring structure and predictability to the child's day and provide comforting expectations.

Since feeling safe and loved are the essential elements of emotional strength and stability, it is also important to provide adequate attention, affection and reassurance. The situation may require that very anxious youngsters sleep in their parents' room until they can comfortably return to their own.

Young children are still in the process of learning to distinguish between reality and fantasy. Therefore, exposure to television should be cautiously limited. When certain graphic images and upsetting news footage is seen, parents must be available to mediate, discuss and diffuse the intensity of these images. Anchor this viewing for children by helping them to differentiate what is real from what is not and providing assurances for their own personal safety and protection.

School-Aged Children: Like both their younger and older siblings, a preoccupation with the details of a terrorist event may be evident in the conversations and interactions of school-aged children for the weeks and months following an attack. As increasingly independent six to eleven-year-olds, these youngsters may demonstrate new regressive behaviors; needing to stay close to parents, being unable to fall asleep alone and experimenting with "babyish" attention-getting behaviors. Fixation on terrorists and the pain that they caused may interfere with children's concentration and attention, as well as their participation in many familiar daily activities like chores, sports and homework.

A terrorist attack provokes anxiety related reactions. Exposed children may have difficulty communicating affection and may become more irritable, angry and aggressive than they had been, previously. Since the predominant themes of children's TV and video-influenced fantasy play emphasize aggression and retaliation, sounds and television images can all trigger specific memory "snapshots" and make a child feel nervous without warning. These anxious thoughts and "flashbacks" can last for many weeks after a traumatic event.

Sometimes a child's brave exterior, which lasts throughout the day, crumbles as night falls. These children require a parent's support to handle a distressed and teary child. Common responses at this age can also include nightmares, difficulty in following directions and paying attention. Fears and anxieties are the underlying cause of a variety of physical symptoms and psychosomatic complaints such as sweating, heart palpitations, headaches and stomachaches. Sleep and appetite disturbances also reinforce these physical problems.

Helping School-Aged Children Cope With Their Fears: Parents will find that monitoring children's television viewing—particularly, limiting exposure to TV news reports—will be critically important. Televised images of a terrorist attack can heighten children's concerns and create further stress. The event is frightening and seemingly occurs, continuously, on the TV news. Since additional reinforcement of the frightening footage is extremely upsetting and serves no informational purpose for youngsters after several airings, reducing the amount of media exposure will, in turn, diminish anxiety.

Keep routines in place and encourage a return to normalcy as soon as possible. Continue a child's household responsibilities without placing extreme pressure on performance. The structure, although difficult, will be comforting. At the same time, attention can be drawn to safety planning and the confidence and security that preparation for a future situation can bring.

Parents can be helpful in encouraging open discussions about terrorism and answering as many of their children's questions as possible. Parents should strive to provide accurate information and relate facts to particular concerns and worries that children may have. Care should be given not to add additional apprehension or volunteer more information than the child needs or has actually requested. During this discussion, parents can share their own concerns, but should also reassure children, once again, that they will do everything in their power to keep their families safe.

Adolescents: The teen years are filled with expectations about the future, a desire for independence and a fervent need for the approval of their peers. A terrifying experience, however, may deposit adolescent children back several steps to previous, more immature forms of behavior.

Living through a terrorist attack during a developmental period of risk-taking and feelings of invincibility can create a particularly confusing and unpredictable time for a teenager. A traumatic event threatens feelings of security and the stability of relationships. Teens need to know that their anxieties and fears are normal and will be tolerated by their peers. The inability to share this enormous burden with trusted friends can cause isolation and leave the child feeling angry and unworthy. The adolescent's feelings of inadequacy and embarrassment may lead to "showing off" and can escalate to reckless behavior.

The adolescent's new sense of vulnerability and fear can come into direct conflict with an emerging self-image of "coolness", fearlessness and recklessness. The young teen's need to feel independent doesn't quite fit with his or her inability *to be just that* - at this time. However, like their moods and behaviors, reactions to trauma can be very intense. Common responses of teens in distress range from agitation or irresponsible "acting out," to seclusion, apathy and depression. These internal struggles are compounded by external realities—like war and terrorism - that are also frightening and unpredictable.

Affected by many physical and emotional changes, adolescents may already feel out of control with both their bodies and their behavior. When the world is also perceived as unstable and out of control, these children can feel helpless and need guidance and support. If this emotional strife leads to lowered self-confidence, it could also signal increased experimentation with alcohol, drugs and other behaviors that make teens feel "cool" and powerful. At times of distress and limited structure, teenagers may show increased risk-taking behaviors and behave in ways that could, potentially, put them at risk.

Helping Adolescent Children Cope With Their Fears: Because teens know more than their younger siblings, they may also worry more. But, they will benefit from the opportunity to be making a positive contribution and feel part of "the solution". Whether clearing debris from the site of a natural disaster or volunteering with the Red Cross, participation in community rebuilding allow these youngsters to feel capable and needed.

It is important to lead adolescents to focus on positive values and see the merits and heroic actions taken by their own friends and neighbors. In doing so, it will help them to downplay their own worries and will be a distraction from persistent concerns about risk and harm. Outreach and pro-social participation support "solution-based" activities and reinforce an adolescent's connections with a larger group and a valuable shared goal.

WHAT PARENTS CAN DO FOR THEMSELVES

Think back to the flight attendant holding up the oxygen mask and directing passengers traveling with children to, "Secure the mask over your own nose first, *before* securing the mask of your child". Surely, helping children cope with an emergency compels parents to be alert, ready and informed before they can completely comfort and safeguard their children. Particularly, when dealing with the many facets and unknowns of a terrorist attack, parents will need to communicate the most up-to-date information and confident manner and be as effective—and as helpful—as possible. Therefore, first attend to your own basic needs; become educated and prepared and stay healthy. Deal with your own personal stress and prioritize your activities—attending to what is really important and not sweating the "small stuff".

Expand your personal "parenting best". Allow your strength and courage to shine through for your family, as they will look to you as a role model for behavior and action. Your bravery and composure will be a powerful predictor of their ability to persevere and cope. Conversely, if you appear to be overwhelmed with anxiety and fear, your child's recovery may be more difficult and drawn out.

A helpful peer group of individuals with common values and concerns as well as similar parenting responsibilities can be a great source of strength and reassurance. Do not wait for an emergency, however, to cultivate this supportive network of neighbors, friends and relatives. Concentrate on those individuals, thoughts and opportunities that provide you with positive energy and leave you uplifted. Simplify your life and stay "in control" by restricting your efforts to only your top priority activities, focusing on only those tasks that are timely and absolutely necessary.

HOW PARENTS CAN HELP CHILDREN COPE WITH ADVERSITY AND TRAUMA?

Parents have a profound effect upon children's ability to manage fear and adversity. During a time of crisis, parents can instill feelings of self-worth and competency that will enable their children to emerge, resilient, from even the most challenging situations. Here are some practical tips to guide this process:

- Be hopeful and optimistic during your family conversations. Explain that the uncertainty your children may feel about the future will surely diminish over time.

- Don't force your children to discuss the details of the terrorist event until they are ready to do so.
- Provide accurate and honest information, but don't burden your family with your own worst-case scenarios or unnecessarily negative or gloomy details of terrorism.
- Children will repeat the same details or ask the same questions over and over. This is simply a technique for gaining your attention and reassurance and deserves your answers and attention. Treat these questions as valid and important observations.
- Focus on solutions and the people providing them instead of the causes and problems surrounding terrorism.
- Learn about trauma reactions and share this information with your family. There is comfort in knowing what to expect and what is considered within the normal range of reactions.
- Keep to established routines and schedules. Familiar rituals will reassure children and help them to feel secure.
- Initiate conversations and encourage your children to speak up and discuss their fears.
- Reinforce the fact that pro-active safety operations are in place and that "first responders", police, fire, hospital workers and many, many others are standing by ready to help them.
- Reassure your family that you will take care of them and that their fear and sadness will, eventually, go away.
- Encourage your children to retain some control over their lives by offering opportunities to make independent and age-appropriate decisions and to handle daily responsibilities.

The American Academy of Pediatrics (AAP) advises parents to establish open lines of communication during an emergency situation. They suggest the following:

- Given what children may have seen on television, they need to know that the violence is isolated to certain areas and they will not be harmed. Parents should try to assure their children that they've done everything they can to keep their children safe.
- Overexposure to the media can be traumatizing. It's unwise to let children or adolescents view footage of traumatic events over and over. If possible, youngsters should not watch these events alone.
- Discussion is critical. It should be stressed that terrorist acts are incidents of desperation that may have been committed by evil individuals who are members of a particular group or shared background. However, most people in a particular group or from a specific background are not terrorists. Nor are they evil or "bad" people.
- Following a trauma, many adults and children have found that it is helpful to talk with a counselor who has specialized training in posttraumatic reactions and can help understand and deal with their emotions. Seeing a counselor does not mean that a child is "mentally ill" or that you have failed to support him or her."

WHAT ARE CHILDREN'S REACTIONS TO TRAUMA?

Following the terrorist strikes in New York and Washington, DC on Sept.11, 2001, a number of large studies were conducted concerning children's initial reactions to trauma. Although the great majority of these children were not in *direct* danger or in physical proximity of the attacks—there were strong similarities among many children's initial reactions. Remarkably, almost all of the children in the study had become "virtual victims" of trauma due to television news exposure of the terrorist attacks.

Regarding this secondary, "virtual" exposure, many children shared the following reactions:

Shock: Children reported that upon first hearing about the terrorist strikes or seeing them on television, they felt shock, disbelief and detachment. Many independently described the experience as like being "inside a video game" or in an action movie.

Fear: Days and weeks after the terrorist strikes, children remained in a state of anticipation and anxiety expecting the "other shoe to drop" and waiting for something else to happen. In addition to being hurt or killed, other serious and unspoken fears included the death of parents and the possibility of being left alone.

"Generalized" Fear: Children throughout the country had anxiety reactions about going into buildings that "reminded them of the Twin Towers in New York." But, for some children, this fear generalized into going into *any* office building or into anxiety about their parents going to work or even leaving the house.

Guilt: Since many children engage in "magical thinking"—leading to the belief that by fantasizing about an event, one can cause it to happen—large numbers of children experienced guilt that, in some way, they were responsible for the attacks. These youngsters were mired in an illogical but common childhood misimpression that by "wishing for" or imagining something - one could actually cause it to happen. Some children had guilt for not being able to prevent the attacks and, still others interpreted the strike as a punishment for something bad they had done or said.

Anger: Even if children were not, directly, affected by the attack, a secondary outcome (i.e. soccer practice being cancelled because of a special assembly *about* the terrorist attack), may have personalized the event and focused "Why me?" anger. Not surprisingly, many youngsters directed their anger for numerous unrelated events toward the "evil terrorists" whom, they believed, caused or prevented other outcomes.

Physical Distress: Physical symptoms such as headaches, nausea, heart palpitations and insomnia were common physical reactions to terror reported by children. The stress and anxiety of a traumatic event may cause similar physical reactions in children and adults.

Panic: Terrorism is unpredictable. Therefore, it is not surprising that large numbers of children reported feeling "out of control" and panic-stricken. These feelings of loss of control and panic occurred in waves and also reoccurred in dreams.

Delayed Reaction: Some children showed no immediate reaction to the terrorist attacks. However, under the surface, many of these youngsters were found to be in a "hyper-alert," vigilant and nervous state.

POST-TRAUMATIC STRESS DISORDER (PTSD)

All children and adolescents experience stressful events that can affect them both emotionally and physically. Their reactions to stress are usually brief, and they recover without further problems. Most children, even those directly exposed to trauma, are amazingly resilient and are not significantly impeded in the course of their lives. However, after the initial shock of a trauma has worn off and things *seem* to be back to normal, some youngsters experience Posttraumatic Stress Disorder (PTSD). This condition rarely appears at the time of the trauma itself, but becomes evident within weeks—and sometimes months - after a traumatic episode.

Post-Traumatic Stress Disorder (PTSD) is a psychological condition that follows a traumatic event. It usually builds quietly over a period of weeks or months and may become a chronic, obsessive disorder. PTSD in children is an intense emotional response to thoughts and reminders of a trauma during which a severe injury, emotional pain or terrible shock has occurred. A child's risk of developing PTSD is related to several things, including the seriousness and closeness of the trauma, whether the incident is repeated and the child's relationship to other victims.

Following a terrorist attack—even if it is something only seen on the TV news—a child's behavior may be significantly affected. A child may show intense fear, helplessness, anger, sadness, or even denial in the wake of a real incident. They may even seem numb to the pain and trauma of the event. Some children will dissociate themselves from the reality of the event, others will become less responsive, depressed, withdrawn, and detached. Each child will experience the occurrence slightly differently and many will relive the emotions of the trauma over and over.

It is interesting to note that numerous children experienced PTSD following the traumatic events of September 11th, even though many of those affected were "virtual victims" - exposed only to television reports of the disaster. For many youngsters, the help of a qualified professional to discuss and minimize the negative effects of the stressful incident was indicated.

The symptoms of PTSD fall into three broad categories:

- **Symptoms of *re-living*** include flashbacks, nightmares, and extreme emotional and physical reactions to reminders of the event. Emotional reactions include having guilt about surviving, as others did not, as well as the numbing of other emotions. Physical reactions include shaking, chills or heart palpitations when thinking about the event.

- **Symptoms of *avoidance*** include staying away from the people, places and things that are reminders of the trauma. A phobic reaction can occur where there is an avoidance of specific activities such as travel on certain dates, or wearing certain color clothing that connects a memory or circumstance with the traumatic event.

- **Symptoms of *increased arousal*** include a state of "over alertness" and an inability to relax. It also includes being easily startled and overly vigilant in preparation for something to happen. Difficulty sleeping and an inability to concentrate or complete daily tasks are characteristic of this "hyper aroused" and agitated state.

PTSD was traditionally associated with soldiers returning from combat with serious flashbacks of war-related horrors. However, certain aspects of this condition have been noted in youngsters who have witnessed or experienced trauma.

Children with Post-Traumatic Stress Disorder may have symptoms for several months to many years after a traumatic event. Overcome by worry, some youngsters seem unable to "shake" the feeling of being vulnerable, powerless or out of control. Persistent recollections and flashbacks of an incident are considered similar to those reported by soldiers upon return from combat, except that many of our young victims are only in front of a television.

With regard to PTSD, parents should be aware of behavioral changes that may significantly interfere with a child's daily life. These may include one or more of the following:

- The development of new fears and phobias.
- Feeling emotionally "blah" and unable to experience joy.
- Increased separation anxiety and clingy behaviors
- Fear of the dark and sleep disturbances
- Worry about death and dying
- Panic attacks
- Pre-suicidal feelings (that the "...world would be better off without me in it")

- Repetitive, obsessive behaviors
- Increased fear about safety; their own and that of their parents

Support from parents, school, and peers are an important part of a consistent, calm and reassuring intervention. Since extreme separation anxiety and nervousness are characteristic of the disorder, parents should do everything possible to minimize their child's anxiety and establish a safe, secure and predictable environment as well as a comfortable routine.

TREATMENT OF POST-TRAUMATIC STRESS DISORDER

Children with PTSD can be treated with a combination of play and creative arts therapy, as children communicate and interact through the forms of expression that they know best for the relief of both anxiety and depression. Encouraging the child with PTSD to speak, write or draw about a particular experience or event can also be beneficial. It can serve as the basis for important conversations and positive therapeutic play opportunities. Behavior modification and talk and play therapy have been successfully used to reduce fears and diminish obsessive and compulsive thinking and behaviors in children with trauma-related emotional problems.

Another approach to treatment with children showing signs of the disorder is cognitive behavioral therapy. In this type of therapy, children are taught methods of overcoming anxiety by learning practical behaviors to manage specific fears. Children are trained not to extend their fears or expect bad things to happen just because something very bad has occurred in the past.

In some instances, medication may be recommended to deal with Post-Traumatic Stress Disorder's severe agitation, anxiety and depression.

As might be expected, parents' responses to a traumatic event can strongly influence their children's reactions and their ability to recover from PTSD. Anxious and depressed parents of young children often, unwittingly, intensify their children's PTSD symptoms. Children will look to parents and close adults for models of appropriate behavior and reactions. Therefore, when parents act distraught and overwhelmed, children may interpret the present danger as uncontrollable. These parents would benefit from professional help and their children would also gain a sense of additional self-confidence in an environment of increased emotional availability and stability. The security that parents provide at this time will have an enduring impact on their entire family's emotional well-being.

With diversions, fun activities and new, predictable routines, parents can create different patterns of behavior and establish new traditions and memories on which to build. Parents who have an awareness of their children's PTSD should seek out new collective experiences and activities around which new supports and traditions can be established and nurtured.

HELPING CHILDREN COPE BY FOSTERING RESILIENCE

Some youngsters seem to be naturally "resilient" and can endure great difficulty, danger and even tragedy. These children are able to move along with their lives tapping into their own, personal reservoir of confidence and determination. Despite their personal losses or disappointments, these fortunate children seem to withstand and overcome adversity—often emerging even stronger by the process. But other children are less able to "pick up the pieces", hold their heads high, maintain their focus and move ahead with the same ease and determination.

The skills that enable resilient children to cope with stress and manage fear are reinforced by their self-esteem, confidence and ability to empathize with others. Psychologists tell us that in the same way that eating well and exercising can, over time, condition the body for good health—supportive relationships, self-reliance and positive reinforcement for small accomplishments can help all children to become resilient and build up a reserve of courage and confidence.

Families can make sure that the underpinnings of this resiliency will support the child's all-around development. These supports begin with the significant connection and trust of others, particularly parents or caregivers. Cultivating resilience compels children to feel competent, powerful and take ownership of their feelings.

Parents may wonder how to demonstrate these behaviors and model resiliency to their kids. One way is for adults to dig back into their own childhoods, and share an incident, with their children, during which they felt scared or rejected—but found something positive to focus upon. Or, parents can retell stories—in concrete terms that a child can relate to - of a brave friend or relative who faced a disease, divorce or other difficulty and rose past this adversity to find strength and get beyond a troubled situation.

Tales of the remarkable courage that was shown by rescue workers, doctors, hijacked passengers and many other "ordinary citizens" after the terrorist attacks of September 11, 2001 continue to resonate with American families. Parents can use this event and many other historical occurrences from slavery to the Holocaust to the Space Shuttle disaster to demonstrate how pain and adversity can be overcome—and can even make people stronger.

The National Institute for Trauma and Loss in Children recommends that parents follow these simple principles when dealing with youngsters following a traumatic incident:

- Be Protective
- Be Patient
- Be Nurturing
- Be Consistent
- Be Informed

FAITH TO COPE WITH WAR AND TERRORISM

Sharing religious beliefs with your children can lift their spirits and promote emotional healing. In a time of uncertainty and stress, many families find comfort and strength in their faith and traditions. Faced with war and threats of terrorist attacks, Americans of every religious and spiritual tradition will search for the best ways to help their families move forward with their lives. Particularly in times of crisis, many parents will look to their faith for that support and guidance.

For many, fear challenges their emotional and physical sense of well being as well as their spirituality. As a result of fear and adversity, however, many families will rely on faith, prayer and meditation to seek reassurance and understanding. Along with the tragic circumstances, children will also need opportunities to celebrate the good and fortunate aspects of their lives. Religious services and gatherings can help to identify positive life forces and good behaviors and emphasize goodness, kindness and hope.

RECOVERY THROUGH HELPING AND ACTION

Another strategy for reducing children's fear and stress is to assist them in concentrating their anxiety and concern towards positive action. This action can range from something very simple, like a smile or a phone call to becoming a volunteer. By giving children responsibilities and opportunities to participate in helping and recovery activities, they will feel more in control and better about themselves.

Pro-social actions, even when they are not directly linked to a specific event, help children feel positive about the future and hopeful about their own circumstances. Following a traumatic event, doing something kind for an elderly neighbor or caring for a sick animal can help the child to focus outside of himself and feel empowered to have a positive effect upon the world.

FAMILY PLANNING: A COMPREHENSIVE DISASTER PLAN

Although government documents often refer to terrorism's "first responders" as firemen, policemen and emergency room physicians, in reality, parents are—and will always be—their children's "first responders" in the event of a major assault. If there should be a terrorist attack, it will, most likely, occur without any warning. Therefore the best way to prepare is to *be* prepared—and have a family "emergency plan" in place. These procedures need not be elaborate, but they should be specific. Shared plans should include emergency contact numbers; identification information, family meeting locations and a well-stocked disaster supply kit. Collecting this material and organizing supplies will not cause additional anxiety in children. In fact, family members will be relieved to know that a blueprint for dealing with disasters and other emergencies - before such events ever occur - is firmly in place. Having some detailed information about simple plans to be implemented following an emergency on hand can provide comfort, a feeling of control and a sense of safety. Here are some of the fundamental items to be incorporated into your family emergency plan:

- ***Meeting places:*** Select and discuss potential meeting places where family members will be sure to find each other following a disaster. Determine two different areas; one right outside your home, so all will be immediately aware of who is still inside the house; and another, away from your immediate neighborhood, in case an emergency prevents you from being in the immediate area of your home.
- ***Escape routes:*** Plan and practice escape routes from your home, particularly from bedrooms.

- ***Family contacts:*** Designate a friend or relative to be your "family contact" to make sure all family members will have a single point of contact. Suggest that children know this person's name and number as well as e-mail address or other contact information.
- ***Alternative location:*** Should a crisis occur while your child is at school, select a location near the school where all members of the family can meet.
- ***Important phone numbers:*** Have children note or memorize "important" numbers and also place this information near each phone in your home. Numbers that should be included are:

  911 (or other emergency numbers)
  Telephone number of children's school(s)
  Telephone number of your work
  Telephone number of neighbor(s)
  Telephone number of "family contact"

- ***Pets:*** Make sure your pets are current on their vaccinations and that there is a plan in place for them to travel with you or be sheltered elsewhere, if necessary.

Since preparedness for any catastrophic incident involves organization as well as common sense, you may want to have the following items on hand in a prearranged location:

- Food and water for several days
- Blankets / Pillows, etc.
- Warm and dry clothing

- Medicines
- Personal and legal documents
- Toys, books and games
- Flashlight
- Radio
- Cash
- Current photograph

WHAT IS THE FIRST THING THAT WILL HAPPEN FOLLOWING A TERRORIST ATTACK?

Of course, it is impossible to predict exactly what will occur should there be an act of terrorism. Becoming more knowledgeable about potential scenarios, however, will help parents be less fearful and better prepared to act, should such an event occur.

If a massive, hostile terrorist event should take place, local police and emergency coordinators on radio and television will provide updated information regarding the extent ("code red" or "severe" terror alert) and information about what may be known about the type (destructive multiple-explosions, chemical, biological or nuclear weapons) of event that has taken place.

As additional information becomes available, instructions related to emergency safety responses, specific to the location and category of attack, will be given. Sheltering options most often recommended are 1) communal sheltering, outside of the home, 2) "in-home" safe room or sheltering place or 3) impromptu "sheltering *in* place", if the population is instructed to remain right where they are and create appropriate "shelter" in that place.

Some parents will want to create shelter in their own homes. This interior "safe room" is somewhat modeled after the bomb shelters of the 1950's and the stylized "panic rooms" of some "high-tech" mansions built in the 1990's. An appropriate space for such use is an interior room or a basement area with as few openings as possible. If feasible, a room connected to a bathroom is most suitable. The following items should be stored in that room for use in an emergency:

- First aid kit
- Food and bottled water
- Flashlight
- Battery-powered radio and extra batteries
- Duct tape and scissors.
- Towels and plastic sheeting
- Phone

Should it be necessary to shelter your family at home for several hours following a terrorist attack, covering windows in this "safe room" with a plastic sheet and creating an unbroken seal with duct tape around the windows and doors may provide some increased protection against air-delivered chemical agents. Of course, it is critical to make sure an adequate air supply remains in the room. Although this type of seal may slow down the movement of air from outside to inside, it will not stop such movement, entirely. Air conditioners and fans that circulate air should be turned off and fireplace dampers, hatches and other openings to the outside, closed.

WHAT IF IT'S A BIO-CHEMICAL ATTACK?

In the very remote possibility of a bio-terror strike, it is likely that we will not know that an attack has occurred right away. In fact, we will probably be unaware of this type of strike until certain medical symptoms begin to bring people to hospital emergency rooms and doctor's offices. As similar symptoms are noticed and a particular medical pattern and causal agents become evident, linkages to the category and location of the bio-weapon used will become apparent.

Careful lists called "medical surveillance registries" will link together people and their specific symptoms until a clear picture emerges regarding the number of people affected. Affected individuals, their locations, strength of their symptoms and incubation periods will all be monitored. These information clusters will be key in tracing the type and probable location of the initial exposure and specific biological agents responsible. Sophisticated computer data-bases will enable responders and hospitals to monitor and predict where outbreaks within the population will occur.

One of the most horrific—and difficult realities—of a bio-terror attack is the fact that children are particularly vulnerable. Children are more sensitive to the airborne exposure of biological and chemical weapons than their parents and have faster and more absorbent respiration than do adults. A larger surface of skin for exposure and more skin cuts and open scrapes through which germs and chemical spores can enter the body make younger, smaller individuals, more susceptible to biological and chemical organisms than adults.

Although bio-chemical agents affect adults and children in similar ways, children's adverse reactions and allergies to the antibiotics used to counteract the exposure also may interfere with eradicating the damaging effects of these agents. In addition, threats to theme parks and schools may indicate that merciless terrorists may specifically target innocent children.

In the event of a bio-terrorism incident, the safety of the members of your family will be determined, primarily, by their individual proximity to the point of the weapon's release and the direction of movement of airborne chemicals. Staying out of harm's way will be very much a function of luck in combination with the nature and characteristics of the contamination and the availability of specific vaccines, remedies and treatments.

The CDC (Centers for Disease Control and Prevention) suggests that among the biological agents most likely to be used in a terrorist attack are Anthrax and Smallpox. These toxic agents are particularly threatening because a small "crop duster" airplane or even a perfume atomizer can distribute both Anthrax and Smallpox into the air and cause large numbers of deaths. In contrast to chemical and nuclear weapons that cause immediate destruction and tragedy, illnesses caused by these agents will, generally, not be noticed for some time. Release of the Anthrax bacteria, for example, may not be evident for, perhaps, 24 hours following exposure. Smallpox symptoms may not be apparent to victims for almost 2 weeks after initial infection.

Anthrax: *Bacillus anthracis* is the bacteria-causing agent of Anthrax. In its various forms, Anthrax can contaminate skin, be inhaled into the lungs or even be digested with food. Anthrax bacteria are found in nature in tainted farm animals and some of their products. An Anthrax infection could occur following contact with contaminated animals or their infected parts (such as fur, bones, wool, hides, or leather).

Anthrax thrives in warm-bodied creatures and can even stay potent for years outside living things - in soil, for instance - by creating a protective surface coat or "spore". Should these spores become widely disseminated, they could enter a person's body and quickly become living bacteria that deliver poisonous toxins. Anthrax spores can enter the body and release lethal substances in the following ways:

- ***Cutaneous Anthrax*** (entry through the skin) shows symptoms on the skin within 1-2 days after exposure. This is the most common form of the Anthrax infection and occurs when the bacteria enters a cut or abrasion on the skin. Contact causes itchy, raised sores and open lesions. The Anthrax toxins kill skin cells beginning with a wound that looks like a spider bite. The sore becomes ulcerated and later dries with a black heavy scab.
- ***Inhalation Anthrax***, (entry through the lungs) is transmitted by simply breathing in, but may take up to 60 days for symptoms to appear and for Inhalation Anthrax to be diagnosed. Beginning like the flu, breathing becomes increasingly labored and quickly progresses to severe respiratory failure. If Anthrax is "weaponized" into fine particles and disseminated in an aerosol form through the

air, this infection could be widely spread before the population has a chance to avoid breathing in its poison.

- ***Intestinal Anthrax*** (entry through the stomach) appears between 1 and 7 days after Anthrax spores are consumed in food. Naturally occurring exposure of the bacteria usually follows the consumption of raw or contaminated meat or dairy products. Undercooked, contaminated food that carries the bacteria causes fever, gastric distress and severe diarrhea.

There are several emergency procedures that your family can utilize to decrease the severity of potential contamination from Anthrax. Should there be exposure to the Anthrax spore, quick action can help your family avoid the most severe reactions to the bacteria:

- Leave any area that has been exposed to Anthrax spores immediately.
- If Anthrax spores have been dispersed into the air, your family should cover their mouths with wet wash cloths or respiratory masks and try to hold their breath or take shallow breaths.
- Remove outside clothing and all items that have, potentially, been exposed to spores. Place these items in plastic bags and double seal them. Since they are contaminated, leave these bags and do not take them with you.
- Wash thoroughly with soap and hot water.
- Begin treatment, as recommended by the Department of Health, with antibiotics—including Ciproflaxacin ("Cipro"), Penicillin, or Doxycycline—prior to the onset of symptoms.

Smallpox: Like its name derived from the Latin word for "spotted", the raised white bumps and extensive rash that is characteristic of Smallpox covers the body in a horrific blanket of bumps. Caused by the variola virus, Smallpox is highly contagious and often fatal. Smallpox has been virtually eliminated from the planet, with no documented cases in the United States for over fifty years.

However, in the aftermath of the events of September 11, 2001, concern that the *variola* virus could be used as a weapon of bio-terrorism has increased U.S. public health vigilance about a potential reappearance of Smallpox. To meet this possible threat and its terrible consequences, a nationwide Smallpox response and vaccination program has been designed and a stockpile of Smallpox vaccine for emergency intervention has been assembled. In the very unlikely event that this virus was to be released in a terrorist act, the American public could quickly be vaccinated and an outbreak averted.

Although the Smallpox vaccine is considered safe, it is not without side effects and complications. This is particularly true for individuals with certain pre-existing immune disorders and heart conditions. Young children may be considered at risk for adverse reactions, so vaccinations should only be considered in light of a significant and immediate Smallpox threat. Other antiviral agents are being tested to combat the variola virus, including a new drug called Cidofovir.

The viral particles that spread Smallpox travel through small airborne droplets that are inhaled following close contact with an infected person or contaminated object. Once breathed in, small sores develop in the mouth, throat and, eventually, cover the skin. After exposure, it takes between 7 and 17 days for symptoms to appear which will include high fever, head and body aches, vomiting and an extreme, bumpy rash that starts on the face and spreads to the arms and legs. Vaccination within 3 days of initial contact with the virus can prevent the severity of Smallpox symptoms. Even up to a week after exposure, the vaccination may still lesson the symptoms and offer *some* protection against the disease.

Parents should note that Smallpox could actually spread by touching the vaccination site before it has fully dried up and a scab has been created. The live virus collects in the open lesion formed over the vaccination. Therefore, contact with the site or any material, bandage or fabric that has come into contact with it should be avoided. Careful washing of hands each time the area is touched is essential.

WHAT IF IT'S A CHEMICAL ATTACK?

Chemical weapons will act within seconds or minutes on the human body, damaging the body's exposed and underlying tissue. The CDC suggests that among the chemical agents the population should be familiar with is the blistering agent, Mustard Gas. Knowing about Mustard Gas and how quick reactions will help diminish its lethal capability may be life saving information for families.

Mustard Gas has already been used as a chemical warfare agent since the early part of the century and as recently as the Iran-Iraq war in the 1980's.

The release of the toxic Mustard Gas is particularly dangerous because it is almost impossible to detect until exposure has already occurred.

Sulfur Mustard and the Mustard Gas that it emits can have the smell of garlic or "mustard" but often has no odor at all. It can take a variety of forms from that of an invisible gas, an oily liquid or even a solid. Exposure to this toxic chemical can occur from contamination to the gas while near a hazardous materials waste site where chemicals have been discarded, or from the breathing in of fumes during an attack. After release, Mustard Gas can stay potent in the air for several days under average weather conditions. The Sulfur Mustard vapor can be disbursed over dozens of miles as it is carried long distances by wind.

Sulfur Mustard is a powerful irritant and blistering agent that burns and destroys the skin, eyes, and lungs. Direct exposure to the eyes can cause permanent blindness. If inhaled, Mustard gas increases the risk of lung damage and can cause chronic respiratory disease, bronchitis and lung cancer. This exposure can also damage DNA and contribute to birth defects in future generations.

Depending on the severity of exposure, reactions to the chemical, including redness and itching, become evident within 2 to 48 hours after contact. Skin irritation often changes to yellow blistering, particularly around parts of the body where mucous membranes and sweat forms. Direct contact with the chemical liquid can produce second- and third- degree burns and later scarring.

The thorough removal of the Sulfur Mustard from the skin is the only way to avoid tissue damage. Wash all exposed areas of the body with clean water and flush out eyes with plain water for at least 10 minutes. Unfortunately, there is no antidote for the Sulfur Mustard chemicals, so it is important to quickly leave the area of release and remove all clothing that has been contaminated. Seal all exposed materials and clothing in a plastic bag and leave the sealed bag. If at all possible, try to relocate to higher ground, as Sulfur Mustard is heavier than air and tends to settle in low-lying areas.

WHAT IF IT'S A NUCLEAR ATTACK?

Living with the "permanent potential" of terrorist attacks, government officials have voiced concerns about the possibility of radiological weapons falling into the hands of renegade governments, assassins or fanatical organizations as well as the vulnerability of nuclear power plants in our nation's communities. Several "worst case" scenarios include the contamination of the food or water supply; the release of a mixture of conventional explosives, such as dynamite and radioactive materials in small explosive devises ("dirty" bombs or "suitcase bombs"); the explosion of an atomic bomb or the release of radioactive material due to an explosion, meltdown or leak at a nuclear power plant.

In the very unlikely event of the release of a weapon of mass destruction (WMD) or a radiation emergency, an assessment of radiation levels will be broadcast on emergency response networks and news stations. Having a battery-operated radio on hand will be critical in getting information and advice about what protective actions, if any, you will need to take.

Recommendations about what to in such a circumstance will totally depend upon the specific situation and numerous other elements. Although it is impossible to speculate about specific measures that should be taken, there are some general guidelines about life-saving strategies to take during this type of emergency. Most safety experts encourage parents to be aware of three general principles of response to a nuclear event, including shielding, distance and time.

Shielding: Placing as much of a "shield" or barrier between yourself and radioactive materials as possible. This allows greater quantities of the radiation to be absorbed by the barrier so your potential exposure will be less.

Distance: The greater the distance you are located away from a nuclear event and radioactive material, the lesser the chances and/or the severity of exposure.

Time: Limiting the time spent exposed to radiation and absorbing its fallout, the greater the reduction in risk. Even following exposure to radioactive material, each hour of additional exposure can increase the severity of associated illness.

It is reasonable to assume that acting on "shielding" by "sheltering in place," will be beneficial. This will probably involve a short-term stay, as a family, in an interior room or basement of your home. If possible, you should not venture outdoors until there is information assessing radiation levels, wind direction, etc. and you are told it is safe to do so. In a sheltering environment, make sure you have an adequate supply of bottled water and food and all windows and air-conditioners are closed.

If there should be a release of low-levels of radiation, Potassium Iodide (KI) pills will offer some protection from radiation exposure to the thyroid gland, by decreasing the amount of harmful radioactive iodine that can be absorbed by the thyroid. Potassium Iodide guards against the production of some, but not all types of future tumors and cancers. Like exposure to bio-chemicals, children are particularly vulnerable to the effects of radiation. Although Potassium Iodide pills will benefit the later health of youngsters as well as adults, they offer no armor against many other life-threatening effects of radiation.

A mass catastrophe such as a nuclear attack is, perhaps, the most horrific circumstance that any family will ever know. In this emergency, children will look to their parents for information, support and hope during the very trying moments that make up a disaster of such proportions. It is important to honestly acknowledge what is factual about these events as they unfold, but also reassure children that they are loved and that parents can - and will - do everything in their power to keep them safe.

TALKING TO CHILDREN ABOUT WAR AND TERRORISM

Since terrorism - by its horrible nature - is unpredictable, having helpful material on hand to turn to will be crucial for parenting smarter and safer. Here are several useful references:

David Fassler M.D., a child and adolescent psychiatrist, has developed the following recommendations for talking to children about war and terrorism. These tips are also available at www.psych.org

- Create an open and supportive environment where children know they can ask questions. At the same time, it's best not to force children to talk about things until they're ready.
- Give children honest answers and information. Children will usually know, or eventually find out if you're "making things up". It may affect their ability to trust you or your reassurances in the future.
- Use words and concepts children can understand. Gear your explanations to the child's age, language, and developmental level.
- Be prepared to repeat information and explanations several times. Some information may be hard to accept or understand. Asking the same question over and over may also be a way for a child to ask for reassurance.
- Acknowledge and validate the child's thoughts, feelings, and reactions. Let them know that you think their questions and concerns are important and appropriate.
- Be reassuring, but don't make unrealistic promises. It's fine to let children know that they are safe in their house or in their school.

But you can't promise children that there won't be a war or that no one will get hurt.

- Remember that children tend to personalize situations. For example, they may worry about friends or relatives who live in a city or state directly or indirectly associated with terrorist incidents.
- Help children find ways to express themselves. Some children may not want to talk about the thoughts, feelings, or fears. They may be more comfortable drawing pictures, playing with toys, or writing stories or poems.
- Avoid stereotyping groups of people by country or religion. Use the opportunity to explain prejudice and discrimination and to teach tolerance.
- Children learn from watching their parents and teachers. Children will be very interested in how you respond to world events. They will also notice changes in your routines such as reducing business travel or modifying vacation plans, and they will learn from listening to your conversations with other adults.
- Let children know how you're feeling. It's OK for children to know if you are anxious, confused, upset or preoccupied by local or international events. Children will usually pick it up anyway, and if they don't know the cause, they may think it's their fault. They may worry that they've done something wrong.
- Don't let children watch too much television with violent or upsetting images. Ask local TV stations and newspapers to limit the repetition of particularly disturbing or traumatic scenes. Many media outlets have been receptive to such overtures.

- Help children establish a predictable routine and schedule. Children are reassured by structure and familiarity. School, sports, birthdays, holidays and group activities all take on added importance.
- Don't confront your child's defenses. If a child is reassured that things are happening "very far away" it's probably best not to argue or disagree. The child may be telling you that this is how they need to think about things right now in order to feel safe.
- Coordinate information between home and school. Parents should know about activities their child's school has planned.
- Teachers should know about discussions that take place at home, and about any particular fears, concerns or questions a child may have mentioned.
- Children who have experienced trauma or losses in the past are particularly vulnerable to prolonged or intense reactions to news of war or heightened fears of possible terrorist attacks.
- These children may need extra support and attention. Monitor for physical symptoms including headaches and stomachaches. Many children express anxiety through physical aches and pains. An increase in such symptoms without apparent medical cause may be a sign that a child is feeling anxious or overwhelmed.
- Children who are preoccupied with questions about war, fighting, or terrorism should be evaluated by a trained and qualified mental health professional. Other signs that a child may need additional help include: ongoing sleep disturbances, intrusive thoughts, worries, recurring fears about death, leaving parents or going to school. If these behaviors persist, ask your child's pediatrician, family practitioner or school counselor to help arrange an appropriate referral.

- Although many parents and teachers follow the news and the daily events with close scrutiny, many children just want to be children. They may not want to think about what's happening half way around the world. They'd rather play ball, climb trees or go sledding.
- War and terrorism are not easy for anyone to comprehend or accept. Understandably, many young children feel confused, upset and anxious. As parents, teachers and caring adults, we can best help by listening and responding in an honest, consistent and supportive manner.

Fortunately, most children - even those exposed to trauma - are quite resilient. Like adults, they will get through these challenging times and go on with their lives. However, by creating an open environment where kids feel free to ask questions and share emotions, we can help to reduce the risk of lasting emotional difficulties.

GOVERNMENT GUIDANCE

The Homeland Security Advisory System is an updated index of America's current vulnerability to terrorism. Threats of potential terrorism are carefully monitored and assessed by the United States Attorney General and the Secretary for Homeland Security. New intelligence information is continuously updated and communicated to citizens through a color-coded warning system.

Threat conditions and the risks of terrorism include both the probability of an attack and its potential magnitude and severity. The following categories, from low (green) to severe and imminent (red), are reviewed and adjusted daily:

Low Probability (Green) is declared when there is a low risk of a terrorist attack. Measures to be implemented at this time include practice drills and the training of personnel in appropriate responses to the Homeland Security Advisory System.

Guarded Condition (Blue) is announced following increased concern about potential terrorist attacks. In addition to protective measures, a dialogue with emergency response teams should begin.

Elevated Condition (Yellow) warns that a significant risk of terrorism now exists. Parents would be well served to coordinate emergency plans with their local communities and schools.

High Condition (Orange) signals a high alert and a significant risk of a terrorist attack. Protective measures will need to be implemented along with security efforts in partnership with federal, state, and local law enforcement agencies, the National Guard and military reserve organizations.

Severe Condition (Red) is represented by a code "red" and reflects a severe risk of a terrorist act. Assigning emergency response personnel, closing and protecting public buildings and redirecting personnel to activities that address critical emergency needs will occur.

PART II

SCHOOL VIOLENCE

WHAT IF...
MY CHILD IS A VICTIM OF SCHOOL VIOLENCE?

Unlike "horse and buggy" or "roller and coaster" the words "school and violence" were never meant to go together. Just the proximity of these two words to each other is appalling. Yet, violence is a reality on our streets and in our schools.

We can no longer brush off the issue of hostility and bloodshed with "not in my backyard" or "not in *my* child's school". We now know better. Although the primary mission of our schools is to teach our children, without a secure environment for instruction, students cannot learn and teachers cannot teach. Incidents of unspeakable violence have been carried out in the classrooms of Jonesboro and the hallways of Brooklyn. In small towns, urban communities, military bases, alternative communes, reservations and walled suburban enclaves, parents are concerned about the safety of their children and want to do something about it.

Prevention and preparedness are critical if we are to minimize the risk of violence in our schools. Research has shown that school communities can do a great deal to prevent violence and foster appropriate behavior. With a safe and responsive foundation in place, schools can provide a first-rate learning opportunity for all youngsters as well as intervene to offer additional psychological services to those who are still struggling to manage their anger.

Schools that encourage children's successful learning and development have a strong academic focus, support students in achieving high standards, foster resilience and facilitate parental involvement. An effective and safe school should be the hub of activity for a community and a place where children feel a sense of belonging and pride. A child should never feel threatened walking into a lavatory alone or insecure staying after school for help with homework.

Most schools are secure places. However, not all schools are equally safe. National data suggests that middle and high schools, especially larger schools, are more at-risk for serious violence. While shocking and senseless shootings give the impression of dramatic increases in school-related violence, our national statistics do not show these numbers to be significantly on the rise. So, while we can take some comfort in the knowledge that schools are relatively safe, we cannot be complacent until they are 100% violence free. The loss of one child to a meaningless act of school violence is one too many. What if it were your child?

WHERE DOES SCHOOL VIOLENCE COME FROM?

The violence that occurs in our neighborhoods and communities has found its way inside the schoolhouse door. Families must now be committed to reducing the behaviors and attitudes that are precursors to violence and demand that fighting, aggressive bullying and victimization are unacceptable and can not—and will not—be tolerated.

It is often argued that violence is not a 9 to 3 problem—it's a societal "issue". If there is fighting in a school cafeteria or gym, it probably didn't start there. Although the roots of this problem may not be in the basements of school buildings, the trouble that emerges must be addressed within those walls. It is clear that the seeds of school violence are planted and nourished within our families and communities. And, long before children ever enter school, their values have already "taken root".

But, schools are particularly fertile ground for growing aggressive confrontations and incidents of revenge. The outside sources of violence will inevitably impact the school environment. School violence, therefore, is a front burner issue for all citizens and a stunning illustration of our communities' most disenfranchised children and dysfunctional families.

The citizens of Jonesboro, Arkansas; Pearl, Mississippi; Brooklyn, New York; Paducah, Kentucky and Columbine, Colorado know that image all too well. First-hand experience has taught them that in addition to unmitigated rage, easy access to guns has made horrific acts of violence in schools even more lethal.

Because of violence in our schools, children and teachers are nervous and fearful. The lack of predictability, the risk of bodily harm and the inability to control a potentially deadly situation all contribute to great anxiety. In addition to the perceived dangers inside schools, many children report being fearful of attacks on their way to and from school buildings. A recent survey of students found that many reported missing one or more days of classes for fear of personal security.

BULLYING: THE FORCE BEHIND SCHOOL VIOLENCE

Feeling bullied—and wanting to bully—are indisputable antecedents to anti-social behavior in school. Bullying is an issue in its own right, but perhaps more importantly, is a precursor to difficulties with aggressive behavior later in life. Children fear the bully on the school bus as well as the abusive girl at the next locker. Parents, teachers, school administrators and pediatricians are woefully aware of the pervasive and serious public health problem that school violence has generated. As the severity of school violence continues to escalate, an examination of the profiles of a number of the school shooters over the last four years reveals deep concern with being "mocked", "persecuted" or "picked on" by school peers.

About one-third of elementary students report that they have experienced being bullied. Still, many school administrators and teachers underestimate, or are unaware of, the extent of bullying in their classrooms. Many youngsters claim that they have not revealed all incidents because they don't want to be viewed as "tattle tales" by their classmates. Some children have suggested that harassment goes unreported because they don't believe that teachers will take serious action against bullies.

Difficulty in implementing effective programs to eliminate harassment and bullying does not stem from a lack of information about what to do or how to do it. There are numerous programs available that have had success in dealing with anti-social behaviors and reducing the occurrence of bullying in schools. Rather, the problem seems to be one of awareness that victimization by bullies *is a serious issue* and one that fosters school violence, confrontation and aggression.

WHO IS THE BULLY AND WHO IS THE VICTIM?

In the past, bullying was thought of as a "mean spirited" but harmless behavior. Bullying-type harassment was often accompanied by justifications such as, "Boys will be boys" or "Sticks and stones can break your bones, but names can never *really* harm you." Even today, when children say or do hostile or hurtful things, these actions are often dismissed as very minor infractions—"rites of passage"—that children will "grow out of". Needless to say, everyone has heard excuses such as:

- "Being bullied builds character."
- "Bullying is part of growing up."
- "What did you do to make him treat you that way?"
- "You just have to toughen up."
- "You just have to learn how to stand up for yourself."
- "Hit him back. He won't bother you again."

- "I was bullied in school and I turned out fine."
- "I was a bully in school and I turned out fine."

These common myths, however, only perpetuate the bully/victim problem. More often than not, a bullying incident will lead a youngster to the principal's office, but rarely, to a counselor or a psychologist.

Bullying is defined as any kind of *ongoing physical or verbal abuse where there is an imbalance of power*—usually a bigger, older child picking on a smaller or weaker one. Bullying also often includes a series of harsh "put downs" and callous "one up-man-ships".

An important distinction between the act of bullying and the normal childhood conflicts and confrontations involved in growing up, is that bullying is uneven. This imbalance creates a situation where one child is hurt or upset (usually the smaller or weaker one) and the other gloats in his superiority. Rather than two counterparts in a squabble or argument, there is a victim, who is made to feel upset, and an oppressor, who regales in being hurtful. Although some conflict between kids is expected, the atmosphere created by bullying should not be tolerated.

An act of bullying can consist of physical, psychological or verbal mistreatment. It can be as direct as teasing, hitting or threatening, or as indirect as starting a rumor, targeting a particular child for retribution or a "stare down". Bullying may seem benign at first, but it usually quickly escalates to overtly hostile behavior. Therefore, it is important that adults do not mistake the behavior for routinely acceptable childhood conflict.

The victims of bullying are typically passive youngsters, often noticed and marked because of an outstanding characteristic—lack of strength, overweight, sexual preference, disability or accent. Boys usually bully smaller, weaker and younger boys and often do so when they are alone. Girls, however, are typically empowered and "egged on" by a group of friends to bully aggressively. Some may "mock" their less confident victims while standing protected by the group.

Not all children are equally likely to be victimized by bullies. Children who are prone to being picked on also tend to have limited social skills and confidence and are caught off guard and afraid. They typically cry easily, or are unable to stand up for themselves. Some children actually seem to provoke their own victimization. But, children who are not bullied tend to have protective social skills and astute conflict management abilities. They are better able to assert themselves and consider alternate solutions. They tend to be more empathetic and shrewd in handling other children and usually can avoid a physical confrontation and resolve a dispute without being victimized.

THE NATURE OF BULLYING

The phenomenon of bullying deserves special attention by educators, parents, and children concerned with violence prevention for two reasons: First, because of the prevalence of bullying which is pervasive in schools today and seriously underestimated and, secondly, because violence prevention strategies can not overlook the predictive link between bullying and the potential for increasingly violent behaviors.

The nature of bullying does not, necessarily, lend itself to the same interventions that may effectively reduce other types of conflict among children. Because it involves harassment by powerful children against children with less power (rather than a conflict between peers of relatively equal status), common conflict resolution strategies such as mediation may be ineffective. Concerned parents and teachers, however, are increasingly alarmed by the climate of aggressive behavior and the damaging consequences that bullying creates as well as the climate of ridicule and intimidation that it has engendered.

Recent research shows that bullying is on the rise and that its delivery has become even more vicious and unkind. Bullying behaviors that appear to be escalating most dramatically; rumors, verbal intimidation, pushing and shoving and spitting, reveal the incivility that many children use to be "cool", powerful and popular against others. Since kids desperately want to be well liked by their peers, it is extremely difficult to go against the group and stick up for the underdog at the expense of one's own popularity.

Bullying among children that "works" to keep certain youngsters powerful and put others down is often emulated. Studies of bullying suggest that there are short- and long-term "dominance" consequences for both the perpetrators and victims of the behavior. Chronic victims of bullying have an increased risk for depression, anxiety and other mental health problems, even into adulthood.

Taunting is a component of bullying that is often subtle and used as a ritual in the harassment of a vulnerable victim. Although some of these interactions can go practically unnoticed by the children around the victim, the bully can clearly see the harmful distress that he or she has caused. Some general characteristics of bullies include observations that they:

- Receive satisfaction from causing humiliation
- Want to feel powerful and in control
- Act impulsively and often recklessly
- Have a low frustration tolerance
- Often have negative attitudes toward school
- Are defiant and oppositional
- Lack empathy
- Are self-righteous and egocentric
- Behave aggressively
- May have been victims of abuse or bullying, themselves

According to the National Association of School Psychologists, about one in seven school children who have experienced constant put downs, threats and bullying may become anxious about going to school and may become school phobic.

YOUR CHILD AND BULLYING

A child is considered to be a victim when he is exposed, repeatedly and over time, to negative actions on the part of one or more other children. Oftentimes, children will not tell their parents that they are being victimized. Avoiding certain situations, people, or places, or pretending to be sick or busy are common maneuvers to avoid bullies. Other behavioral characteristics of victimized youngsters include:

- Fear of going to school
- Fear of using the school bathroom
- Fear of the bus ride to and from school
- Diminished ability to concentrate
- Frequent crying spells and feeling sad
- Recurrent physical symptoms
- Unexplained bruises and injuries
- Anxious or depressed when returning from school
- Experiences mood swings and irritability
- Experiences a decline in school performance

Harassment and intimidation extract a terrible toll on children, and the scars can last a lifetime. Unfortunately, "bullying" is not an uncommon experience for many children growing up. We would all like to "bully-proof" our children and protect them from hurtful assaults by aggressive youngsters. Unfortunately, we cannot be with our children 24-7, nor would that allow them to develop the important problem solving skills and strategies that are necessary for their own independent development.

As a first step, parents should be vigilant about observing changes in children's behavior and demeanor. They need to ask pointed questions as well as walk through the experiences that the child has encountered. And, they need to get information and feedback from the child's teachers.

Children often do not share their harassment experiences with parents because they are either too embarrassed or frightened to do so. And sometimes, a youngster may be unable to label the experience as one of bullying, although they will be able to explain being "picked on" in the cafeteria or fearful of another student on the school bus. Bullying can certainly increase feelings of anxiety, isolation and rejection, and may bring a wave of stress into your child's life. Worry about kids "ganging up" or being made fun of in front of others can also affect learning and squeeze the joy and fun out of the school day.

Many children fall into depression as a result of long-term bullying and school phobia is not an uncommon difficulty. It is also not unusual for a child to spend lunch period in the nurse's office to avoid a cafeteria bully and parents must be sensitive to the "real" reason behind the "reason."

To empower children to deal with bullies, parents should emphasize their children's abilities, competencies and self-worth. Self-esteem is excellent protection against the harassment of a bully, as a confident child is less likely to be victimized. Parents can also help to prevent bullying by facilitating new opportunities for children to build friendships and gain self-confidence. Interventions to prevent bullying are critical as the behavior's harmful and frequently enduring effects on its victims can poison an entire school community.

Developing social skills and the ability to be assertive and defensive in the classroom, cafeteria or schoolyard, empower youngsters to feel more secure. Acting less vulnerable can actually help your child stay safe from intimidation. When parents and teachers partner on behalf of the welfare of children, feelings of safety and security are heightened. Therefore, if you believe that your child is the victim of a bully:

- Encourage him to talk openly about the situation and recognize that this is not being a "tattle tale."
- Reassure him that you will partner with his teachers to protect him and keep him safe.
- Help him to demonstrate self-confidence and assertiveness.
- Provide constructive feedback to help him to understand how his own personality may promote his victimization.
- Cultivate his physical prowess and self-esteem and new peer relationships.

Bullying seems to occur most frequently in the sixth, seventh and eighth grades, in schools in urban, suburban as well as rural areas. It is estimated that over 30% of American teens are involved in bullying—as either a bully, a target of bullying, or both. Since children who bully are at increased risk for juvenile delinquency, anger management challenges and alcohol and drug abuse, and, since harassment of others can signal eventual violent actions, crime and even homicide - the implications of bullying are extremely serious. If you are concerned that your child is bullying or intimidating others, it is important to examine your own behavior and parenting practices:

- Do you often strongly criticize or humiliate your child?
- Do you demand unquestioning obedience?
- Do you use spanking as reinforcement and retribution?
- Is your tone overly critical and self-righteous?

- Have you ever belittled or "put down" your child in conversation?
- Have you ever "given in" to your child when he has been extremely demanding, thereby sending the message that bullying "pays"?

Adult tolerance for bullying or even the inability of some parents and teachers to take it seriously clearly sends the wrong message to children and promotes the implicit acceptability of harassment and humiliation. Exposure to aggressive television programming and films may also reinforce these mean-spirited bullying behaviors by making them seem more "ordinary" and acceptable as well as "effective" in getting what you want.

WHAT CAN YOUR CHILD'S SCHOOL DO?

Every school should be considered "violence free" and "bully free" zones; safe havens with a strong commitment to security, professionalism and a code of ethics. Excellent schools that are concerned about the quality of student life, ultimately, involve all school personnel, as well as the community, students and parents in the creation of a safe and respectful atmosphere. In this ideal setting, rules are communicated to all students and made known to the entire community.

Safe schools strive to eliminate gang violence and bullying episodes by implementing a zero tolerance model. At the same time, these safe schools work toward achieving exemplary diversity and peer relations programs and learning conditions that encourage group interaction and harmony. Adults clearly and consistently communicate that bullying is not acceptable behavior. And, consistency remains the cornerstone of effective violence prevention initiatives.

Determine who is at risk: There are no simple answers to the complex problem of youth violence and, unfortunately, there is no one program, technique or "silver bullet" to remedy the situation, either. Health and social service agencies can provide parents, teachers and school administrators with opportunities to discuss characteristics identified by the National School Safety Center as "potential indicators for a child to commit a violent act and possibly harm him/herself or others."

Awareness of such behavior in a youngster can provide an early warning signal for moving forward with help. This doesn't mean that a particular child is destined to become a violent perpetrator or troublemaker or that he is even capable of anti-social or violent actions. It does mean, however, that extra concern, counseling intervention, referrals for emotional support and supervision and opportunities for successful outcomes in academic and social learning should be provided.

At the same time that potential violence concerns are being addressed, a crisis prevention intervention program should also be developed and a "first responder" safety initiative put into place. The National School Safety Center has suggested that specific behavioral characteristics indicate that a child is, potentially, a risk for instigating a violent episode in school. The Center has expressed concerns about children who demonstrate a cluster of the following behaviors:

- History of uncontrollable angry outburst
- Excessive and angry cursing or abusive language
- Habitual threats of violent retaliation
- History of bringing weapons to school
- Serious disciplinary problems in and out of school
- Predisposition towards drugs and alcohol
- Poor relationships with peers
- Few or no close friends
- Preoccupation with weapons and explosives
- History of truancy
- History of suspension or expulsion from school
- History of cruelty to animals
- Limited supervision or support from parents
- History of abuse or neglect in the home
- History of being bullied
- History of bullying younger children
- Tendency to blame others for problems
- Preference for entertainment with violent themes
- Tendency to write about the dark side of life
- Involvement with gangs or antisocial groups
- History of depression and mood swings
- History threatened and attempted suicide

Children with the potential for violent behavior against others have probably, themselves, been victimized. It is not unusual for youngsters prone to violence to express their own pain when describing their histories of being "picked on" and bullied. Many of these children have had years of impulsive and aggressive encounters and disciplinary, as well as psychiatric, interventions. They are often described as kids "on a very short fuse."

A troubled history is never a clear sign that problems with aggressive behavior or violence will, necessarily, reappear. However, signs that a child may be seriously contemplating harm to himself or others should never be ignored. Recognition of the imminent nature of such behaviors must always be considered. Imminent warning signs should be taken extremely seriously and should be followed up by a referral, an intervention or other appropriate response. Some of these imminent warning signs of violent actions include:

- An escalation in physical fighting with peers or family
- Severe destruction of property
- Episodes of rage
- An escalation in problems and feelings of frustration
- Detailed threats of lethal violence
- Bragging about having weapons and showing them
- Self-injurious behaviors
- Discussion and threats of suicide

Recognizing these behaviors and responding with an appropriate and timely intervention encourages children to eliminate negative behaviors and helps them replace inappropriate actions with positive ones. Active sharing of information and a quick and effective response by the school community will ensure that our schools are safer and our children are safe to learn.

ORIGINS OF SCHOOL VIOLENCE

School violence is not a special strain of terror that exists, exclusively, in the halls of junior highs or in the cafeterias of elementary schools. The origins of school violence are as complex and as multifaceted as the essence of violent behavior, itself. Unfortunately, the rampant cruelty and aggressive conduct that affects schools today is just a tragic extension of what already exists in the broader culture.

There is a large body of research on delinquency and crime that has identified factors linked to the development of school violence. Factors that exist in the home, neighborhood, school, peer group and, of course, within the individual, impact the culture and community of the school and contribute to a climate of school violence. Additional specific problems affecting children and families including child abuse, economic and social deprivation, academic failure, truancy and school dropouts, also play a role in the development of delinquent behavior and school violence.

Obviously, the origin of school violence does not include a single, specific "cause". Nor, is there a single "quick fix" or "special" class, therapeutic program or miracle medication to remedy hostility. There are, however, a number of factors that *contribute* to a youngster's propensity toward violent behavior in school. And, each source and contributing factor can be monitored and addressed by parents, teachers and helping professionals, and interventions for each can occur on both the individual and school levels. Some of those factors include:

Gangs: Gangs and cliques often attract children who are insecure and searching for the acceptance and friendship of a group. When youngsters come together in gangs characterized by violent confrontations, power struggles, rivalries or retaliations, serious problems and potential criminal behavior can occur. Gangs provide dangerous status, as group acceptance often involves "proving oneself" through physical confrontation or aggression.

A group that evolves into a gang may develop a territorial or "school-turf" sphere of influence over school friends and neighborhood peers. Chronic, inappropriate and anti-social behavior and disciplinary problems, if left unchecked, can give rise to some children's tendencies to violate rules, defy authority and participate in increasingly violent, gang-endorsed acts.

A gang offers an identity to a youngster who feels uncertain and powerless by promising gang-membership status and group-identity power. But non-aggressive children who are simply "caught up" in the momentum of the gang's power and status can easily drift into participation in a gang's threatening actions and bullying-like harassment. This implicit approval of gang violence can expand to more dangerous physical violence where moving away from the group becomes increasingly difficult.

Weapons: Guns and other weapons can—and, unfortunately, do—hurt and kill children. Despite a zero tolerance rule for the presence of a weapon on school property, carrying weapons to school has become an acceptable risk for a small but potent number of students.

Some children bring weapons to school to be seen as a "big shot" or to intimidate others by brandishing a firearm. Others believe that violence and intimidation are practical and efficient ways to deal with problems. Still others report they "carry" for protection; although gun-related deaths are the third leading cause of death among children aged 5 to 14 (following auto accidents and cancer) and very steep price to pay for "protection".

Weapons and schools are a terrible combination. Yet more than 40,000 students bring guns into American schools each year. Although it is unlawful to possess a firearm on the property of a school, the increasing presence of weapons in schools has created a threatening, hostile, and fearful climate.

When an environment is filled with anxiety and antagonism, children's psychological and emotional stability can be diminished and violent confrontations are more easily provoked. Obviously, stringent oversight and control of weapons, firearms and all fighting paraphernalia by school personnel is absolutely critical.

Past victimization: Not surprisingly, many children who "act out" in an anti-social way or threaten retaliation for a "wrong" that they claim to have suffered, have themselves been victimized or abused. Abused youngsters are experts in the process of intimidation and victimization. Simply put, children who have been victimized often have the strategies and skills to inflict upon someone else what's already been done to them.

Studies of troubled children with histories of aggressive behavior in home and school reveal over 80 percent of these youngsters were, themselves, victims of harassment, bullying or violence. Perpetrators of violence have often been on the receiving end of abuse—with prominent negative examples available on which to model their own behavior.

Of course, the fact that "violence begets violence" does not excuse violent behavior…nor does it make it more acceptable. The transition from victim to perpetrator of violence is a complex process comprised of modeling, expectations and reinforcement. But this period of transition can also be a time of intervention. The value of early intervention can shed light on the importance of identifying children *prone* to aggressive behavior and designing interventions to benefit these youngsters.

Learning and Emotional Challenges: Many violent acts are committed without forethought or comprehension of potential consequences. For youngsters who are intellectually challenged, emotionally troubled or have difficulty controlling their impulses, the selection of violence can be an all too simple alternative. Impulsivity, inadequate "breaking" skills and limited evaluation techniques can lead to poor choices of behavior. These "high risk" youngsters—particularly those with histories of poor decision-making, fighting, threatening or explosive conduct—need proactive counseling and emotional support.

Learning problems can have a profound effect upon a child's ability to establish friendships, understand consequences and even play games. When a child is challenged in this important area of cognition—be it in problem solving abilities or the understanding of consequences—difficulties arise because social cues and subtle cause and effect relationships may be misinterpreted.

Because learning disabilities and emotional disturbance can result in difficulties in academics, school may bring feelings of inadequacy and poor self-esteem. It may be useful, therefore, to identify children with a poor history of scholastic achievement and limited success in school and intervene with psychological support as well as academic assistance. These youngsters with learning difficulties may benefit from extra emotional comfort and "stress relief" to alleviate the scholastic pressures of competitive schooling. Of course, not every student with learning difficulties feels unworthy or should be labeled as disturbed. But, opportunities for experiencing success in some aspect of school as well as the probability of independent achievement and accomplishments should always be provided.

Just because a child is prone to learning and behavioral challenges, or is often depressed, hyperactive or does poorly in school, it certainly does not mean that he has a predisposition for violent actions—far from it. But, school communities would be well served by a "zero reject" model in which *all* children can successfully contribute something to the workings of the school. This inclusive model of school success does not allow for any student—particularly those with special needs—to become an outright "school failure." When all students are invested in the school process and accepted by faculty and other students, alike, fighting and physical confrontations are reduced.

Neglect: Neglected youngsters may have experienced parental rejection, or simply carry a strong sense of being unloved and neglected throughout their lives. When children feel unappreciated or when poverty and lack of advantages further distance the children from their peers, a youngster's dignity and self-worth is significantly undermined.

Many children may experience low esteem due to neglect and lack of connection with family members. The emotional consequences of such rejection often include a susceptibility to "oppositional reactions" and forceful confrontations. The neglected child may not have developed the resilience necessary to see himself beyond a particular set of circumstances and may view aggressive, acting-out behavior as the only way to obtain recognition. Social service initiatives, in tandem with schools, can help children learn to gain recognition and respect without resorting to violent altercations.

Lack of nurturing mentors: All children benefit by having positive role models and the encouragement and guidance of caring adults. "Pro-social" modeling, for example reduces aggression and fosters cooperation and empathy. Through constructive examples of appropriate behavior and emulating those actions, children can carry out responsible social interactions. Mentors can help children to reinforce those important skills and serve as valuable role models.

As children imitate certain behaviors, they copy them until they become a habit and comfortable action. The single most effective strategy for preventing youth violence is the physical presence of a responsible adult. This is reinforced by numerous studies that show that when children have a meaningful connection to an adult, their potential for violent outbursts is significantly reduced. Role models, mentors and advocates from outside of the home, can all be extremely valuable in making sure that all children achieve their potential.

SCHOOL SHOOTINGS

One person saw his violent website and at least four others heard about the proposed threatened "prank" being planned in honor of Adolf Hitler's birthday. One person heard him actually threaten a teacher...and somebody else knew about his attempts to buy a gun...Independently, these events did not seem significant. But, if the dots could have been connected, a sinister, violent event may have been avoided.

While some incidents of serious violence seem to "come out of nowhere," most occurrences start as less serious disruptions that accelerate into full-scale incidents of violence. Thankfully, the vast majority of these incidents are de-escalated by teachers, administrators or school guards before any one is hurt.

However, with regard to the most feared and publicized of these incidents, school shootings, analysis has shown that in almost every case, the act was not a spur-of-the-moment event, but well planned in advance. According to the U. S. Secret Service's National Threat Assessment Center's study of 37 school shootings, the majority of school "shooters" created their plans of action weeks prior to the incidents. Sadly, many of these youngsters informed and even "boasted" to their friends beforehand about what they intended to do.

Advance knowledge among students about the planned "incidents" of school violence challenges the stereotype that school shooters are "loners" just waiting to "snap". A number of the recent young perpetrators had even discussed detailed "hit lists" as well as suicide plans with several people. Unfortunately, in the vast majority of cases, these threats were never reported to authorities. If warning signs had been relayed, threats reported and information "dots" connected, interventions could have taken place in almost every instance.

Of course, it is not always possible to predict behavior that will lead to violence. This is particularly true of children with no prior record of anti-social actions. However, parents, close family members, teachers and friends can often recognize certain early warning signs. In some situations and for some youngsters certain combinations of events will frequently lead to aggressive rage or violent behavior toward themselves or others. Identifying those children and the combination of events that affect them is crucial.

The National Institute of Justice recently joined forces with the U.S. Secret Service and the U.S. Department of Education to address the issue of school violence and to create a plan to prevent school shootings. They found that in more than three-quarters of the cases examined, the attacker told a friend or friends about his plan. In one case, a school shooter made comments to at least 24 friends about building bombs and murdering students. Findings, compiled in *The Safe School Initiative*, reinforces the need for youngsters to speak up and share any information that they might have regarding possible acts of violence that could be initiated by one of their friends or classmates.

Stereotypes cannot and do not predict who is at risk for becoming violent—and particularly, who might turn out to be a school shooter. Children at risk for severe anti-social behavior cannot be "profiled" as video game addicts or girls who wear sunglasses or boys who wear trench coats. But, there are certain behavioral "risk factors" and warning signs that may be evident and should be addressed, immediately.

When warning signs indicate that danger may be imminent, the safety of the entire school should be the top priority. Immediate actions and interventions must be put into effect by school authorities, students and law enforcement personnel. Early warning signs provide the impetus to check out hunches and enable professionals to intervene before problems escalate. Parents, teachers and all school personnel should be familiar and alert to the range of behaviors that constitute these early warning signs for violence.

Behavioral warnings indicate that a child may need intensive and immediate help. Identifying which behaviors should be addressed and connecting the dots between what a friend has heard, information a parent has shared with a guidance counselor and behavior a teacher has seen in the hallway are the basic building blocks of a safe school. These signs are extremely vital cues to behavior change and could include:

- Withdrawal from social contacts and situations
- Overt signs of depression, rejection, or retaliation
- Communicating feelings of hopelessness
- Communicating that there is nothing to live for
- Intense or recent victimization by bullies
- Prior history of physical or sexual abuse

- Feelings of being picked on and persecuted
- Expressions of hatred in writings or drawings
- Excessive, uncontrollable anger
- Increased intimidation and bullying of others
- Overt prejudice and sympathy towards hate groups
- Increased drug and alcohol use
- Active gang affiliation
- Obsessive interest in weapons

Prior to their murderous rampages, a number of violent children have actually warned or threatened other youngsters about the dangers of being in a specific place at a particular time. These types of statements, particularly when made by disturbed or volatile youngsters, should be taken seriously. They can be a "risk" signal that something is about to occur, particularly when they follow a child's recent history of:

- Serious fighting with peers or family members
- Severe destruction of property
- Severe rage for seemingly minor reasons
- Detailed threats of violence
- Possession and/or use of weapons
- Self-injurious behaviors
- Threats of suicide or homicide
- Abuse of animals

PREVENTION

School violence prevention demands that all schools be prepared for the eventuality of violence. Schools that are safe and responsive have plans and procedures in place to deal with violent and disruptive behaviors, should they occur. Contingency plans for school emergencies are vitally important and necessary and should be developed in the context of an all-inclusive violence prevention plan. Comprehensive prevention plans span areas of academic and psychological support and include components that:

- Reinforce the importance of academic achievement
- Involve families as partners
- Involve the community at every level
- Development of students' talents and interest
- Encourage respectful relationships
- Foster positive student participation at every level
- Address safety issues openly
- Address the dangers of firearms
- Eliminate biases, prejudices
- Offer extended day programs for working parents
- Promote good citizenship, character development

Some students will be successful in learning and behave appropriately in almost any school environment. Other students, however, will require special help or additional support to accomplish learning and behavioral goals. A solid curriculum in social and emotional education can provide all students with the supports and skills they need to become effective learners and problem solvers. In addition, a foundation in the social and emotional needs of youngsters can provide school administration and teaching staff with the skills necessary to foster students' appropriate behaviors and healthy emotional adjustment.

Recently, school violence was labeled a *public health* problem by government and medical agencies. Public health principles and strategies guide community-based approaches to promoting and maintaining safety and the well being of all citizens. With an emphasis on prevention, this approach highlights the risk factors associated with school violence and intervenes with remedies, responses and programs. In the same way that an outbreak of a disease is monitored and managed by public health officials, statistics and programs are now being evaluated to address youth violence. And, just as preventive vaccines are distributed for the outbreak of diseases, sharing effective school safety strategies may be the best prescription for preventing the occurrence of violent behavior in our schools.

LEARNING TO BE SAFE

All children deserve to attend a safe school in which learning and teaching takes place in a supportive and secure environment. All communities deserve schools where responsible student behavior, positive adult examples and fair rules and regulations are followed. Safe schools foster children's growth without worry about violence, intimidation or abuse. The best and safest schools are places where children and learning are the indisputable, top priorities.

Certain characteristics strengthen the framework of schools and guard them against violent patterns of disorder. These "safe school" qualities include:

- Close interaction between parents and faculty
- Strong connections between school and home
- Role modeling of exemplary behavior by faculty
- Emotional support for working with all students
- Innovative teaching practices
- High expectations
- Available opportunities for recognition
- A collaborative spirit
- A focus on academics and developing talent
- Special education and therapeutic services
- Respect for each, individual child

Just as students learn how to write an essay or calculate a math equation, they must also learn how to solve interpersonal conflicts without resorting to violence. A school will have an increased risk of students prone to violence if all students are not encouraged to resolve conflicts and develop problem-solving strategies.

According to the U.S. Department of Education, quality programs share some key administrative similarities and strategies for establishing safe and responsible schools. These include:

- Strong leadership and a caring faculty.
- Family and community involvement and active student participation in the design of programs and policies.
- A physical environment that is safe and school wide policies that promote and support responsible behaviors.
- Prevention and intervention programs that are sustained, coordinated, and comprehensive.
- Intervention programs that are based on student needs.
- Staff that is trained to support and implement programs and approaches.
- Interventions that are monitored and evaluations that are conducted to ensure that the programs are meeting measurable goals and objectives.

One cannot overstate the importance of giving special attention to students who are having difficulty coping with major fears or perceived school failures. When children do not feel empowered and good about themselves, it is difficult for them to feel safe. Although demonstrating a school's commitment to safety can be reassuring and comforting to children, explaining that safety is a shared responsibility involving parents, teachers *and* children can be a powerful and inspiring message.

A cooperative and collaborative relationship between the school, family, community and law enforcement can provide comprehensive groundwork for minimizing the risk of violent behavior in schools. There are a number of supportive strategies that can be implemented to make schools and communities they serve "safer". Here are some of the strategies that work:

Modeling appropriate behavior works: Children learn by example. So, when youngsters see parents fighting with coaches at school sporting events as well as fighting with each other at home, appropriate behavioral messages are severely compromised. Pro-social and appropriate patterns for children's future responses to anger and frustration - including examples that can be emulated - should be provided both in and outside of school. Children must observe adults resolving conflicts with calm words and strategic actions. When children are exposed to models of behavior that are hostile and inappropriate (particularly when they are performed by adults whom they respect) that behavior tends to be imitated as well as validated.

***Limiting Media Exposure works*:** Because of the intensity of their relationships with television and other media, children will be upset and influenced, disproportionately, by exposure to media violence and the reporting of school violence on TV. Aware of increased depression, anxiety and view of the world as a mean and scary place, parents *must* control and restrain children's viewing of violent and anti-social content.

The ability of television news reporting to virtually place youngsters at the scene of a tragedy, particularly one of a school shooting, allows children to practically participate in the action. This degree of immediacy and crisis may be too intense and disorienting for some children and undoubtedly contributes to their feelings of insecurity. Particularly when the surrounding environment is a familiar place, like a school, children are likely to experience extreme vulnerability. They may also project that a news clip seen repeatedly is a violent school shooting, happening over and over again. The world appears to be even more dangerous and menacing than it actually is and schools become places to avoid and fear.

Consistency and discipline work: Safe schools must build their capacity to deal with multiple violations of rules and regulations by developing levels of consequence and penalties. These levels should be systematically followed and both small and major violations addressed with the same fair and consistent approach. Anti-social behavior must be accompanied by discipline and consequences that are understood by all.

Students need to appreciate that the consistent use of incentives and consequences is critical to their safety in school. When previously agreed-upon consequences - such as detentions or suspensions to encourage positive behavior - are not used, students learn that certain inappropriate behaviors may be tolerated.

***Smaller works*:** School safety experts believe that smaller learning communities - like schools within schools, "mini-schools" and assigned home-room classes - are better ways to promote individualized learning and safety than large, impersonal institutions. Smaller learning units tend to have fewer students "fall through the cracks" and foster healthier relationships between faculty and students. Big schools may create additional opportunities for academic coursework and promote more extensive and comprehensive programs from languages to sports. However, research reveals that children profit from individualized attention and favorable relationships with their peers and teachers. Youngsters feel empowered in an environment perceived as smaller, more caring and more manageable.

A team approach works: Looking back at the massacre at Columbine High School, there were numerous signs that perpetrators, Eric Harris and Dylan Klebold were at high risk for violence. The boys had made a home video in which they discussed "gunning down the school jocks". They had written essays and poems for English class about suicide and had posted threats to kill classmates and detonate bombs on their web sites. They were previously seen with weapons in school and their fascination with Nazism was well known. Their histories included psychological problems, social troubles and previous issues with law enforcement.

In retrospect, the potential danger posed by these boys was evident. After the shootings occurred, several classmates of the teens said they were "not surprised" and that the boys were "a time bomb". Unfortunately, however, no one individual saw all of the various elements of risk and was able to connect the dots in time.

The function of a school safety team is to share information and "connect the dots." With regard to safety, teachers, parents, students, social workers, psychologists and law enforcement must all work together to address the potential for violence that certain children present and link their comments, threats, behavior, relationships and associations to the other pieces of relevant information.

School leadership works: School principals and administrators have the responsibility of managing discipline, academics and the training of teachers and staff in modeling appropriate behavior. Clear policy guidelines and thoughtful, consistent supervision build the groundwork for a successful leadership team. Organization is key to enlist the support and participation of parents, teachers and the community in keeping the school environment academically challenging as well as safe. The best and safest schools are in the vanguard of educational systems with crisis intervention plans that are responsive to many types of emergencies. Metal detectors, electronic security screening devices and other technology play a role in supporting a secure physical space. But, strong leadership is the key component of a good academic program, a good athletics program and a good safety program.

Parental involvement works: When revelations that Columbine High School students, Eric Harris and Dylan Klebold had been making shrapnel for bombs in Harris' suburban garage for several weeks prior to their murderous rampage, horrified parents around the country wondered how the parents of these youngsters could not have known what their children were up to. Shocked and concerned, professional organizations, PTA's and communities of faith recommitted themselves to supervision, connection, active interest and involvement in the lives of children. It is clear that supervision is an absolutely essential element of parental responsibility and child and school safety.

Parents must know where their children are, what they are doing and who their friends are at all times. If parents become aware of danger signals in their child's behavior at home—be it constant fighting, verbal threats, cruelty to animals, setting of fires or other anti social conduct, they *must* reach out for help immediately.

Parents are critical to children's school success as well as to their social and emotional adjustment. The partnership between parents and social services at school is necessary, particularly for students who experience behavioral problems at home. At each step in the identification, referral, intervention and treatment process, parents should feel like valued and supported members of a team who can provide an in depth picture of their children's needs, strengths and concerns.

A caring school environment in which children feel attached and emotionally supported allows students to gain a sense of belonging and pride in their school. This connection includes families, children and school personnel and is crucial to the continuance of school safety and security. When each child has a share in the pride and "ownership" of their school's reputation and success, challenging learning opportunities and safe passage are assured.

The University of Virginia Youth Violence Project has developed some helpful recommendations for preventing school violence. These tips are also available on line at <www.youthviolence.edschool.virginia.edu>.

Immediate Actions to Prevent Violence at School

Talk to students about gun violence:

- Acknowledge youth violence as a serious, but preventable problem.
- Explain school policies and safety procedures.
- Obtain student input on their safety concerns.
- Encourage students to report threats of violence.

Identify youth at risk for gun violence at school:

- Students who threaten others or hint about violence
- Students with a history of carrying guns, fighting, destroying property, or cruelty to animals
- Students who are preoccupied with violent fantasies, movies, games, and music
- Students, including suicidal students, who feel rejected, humiliated, bullied, or mistreated.

Take all threats seriously:

- Review student's recent stresses and history of violence.
- Consult with other professionals, estimate risk, and if necessary, take reasonable steps to protect potential victims.
- Develop a plan of action, including non-violence contracts, parent consultation, and follow-up services.
- Assess student's intentions and plans, mental state and motivation.

Long-Term Anti-Violence Strategies

What schools can do:

- Review and maintain clear written policies on school discipline, building security, and crisis response. Enforce school discipline and security policies. Work to maintain a climate of respect for authority and concern for others.
- Initiate school-wide programs starting in the elementary grades to teach student's social competence skills and peaceful methods of resolving conflict. Implement programs to identify and stop bullying.
- Promote student involvement in projects, organizations, and activities, which emphasize non-violence, personal responsibility, and service to others.
- Encourage troubled students to seek help. Use school psychologists and counselors to work with troubled, at-risk students and coordinate efforts with community services.

What parents can do:

- Talk to your children about their problems, fears, and concerns. Take them seriously and give them your support.
- Supervise your children. Know where they are and what they are doing.
- Lock up your guns and ammunition. Talk about gun violence with your children.
- Limit your children's exposure to media violence as a form of entertainment. Discuss with them how media violence desensitizes us to violence and portrays violence unrealistically as a glamorous and effective solution to problems.
- Educate your children in moral values and principles, including personal responsibility and respect for others.
- When in doubt about your child's behavior, consult with school or community professionals.

PART III
ABDUCTION, KIDNAPPING OR EXPLOITATION

WHAT IF...
MY CHILD IS A VICTIM OF ABDUCTION, KIDNAPPING OR EXPLOITATION?

The room was crowded with victim-parents, child advocates and government officials when President George Bush addressed the first White House Conference on Missing, Exploited and Runaway Children in October 2002. "Our society has a duty," he affirmed. "A solemn duty to shield children from exploitation and danger."

With regard to this duty, however, the question remains...are we shielding and protecting our children? And, are we doing all that we can do?

The National Center for Missing and Exploited Children (NCMEC) is the leading organization serving missing and exploited children in the world. The Center has become the "911" for safety services and prevention education as well as a beacon of light for missing children and their families. This chapter is comprised of information, case materials and research compiled over the last twenty years by the NCMEC and reflects the work and wisdom of the Center's experts, Ernie Allen, Nancy McBride, John Rabun, Larry Magid and Tina Schwartz.

CHILD ABDUCTION

> The average victim of abduction and murder is a 13-year-old girl described as an "average" child from a stable two-parent family. Her initial contact with her abductor occurs within a quarter mile of her home...

The kidnapping and murder of a child is overwhelming and terrifying to even consider, as well as an extremely rare event. A *stereotypical* kidnapping, during which a child is taken by an unknown assailant for the purposes of ransoming, harming or holding the child, permanently, occurs about 100 times per year. In approximately half of those horrific crimes, the abduction ends in the murder of the child. An additional 60,000 children per year are victims of *non-family abductions,* kidnapped and illegally held without parental permission by someone who may be known to the child, but does not have legal or family permission to do so and is not a member of the child's immediate family. In about half of these cases, the child-victims seized are sexually assaulted. Over 200,000 additional children are kidnapped by one of their own family members. These *family abductions* usually involve a non-custodial parent who has taken and held their child in violation of legal custody agreements.

If your child is missing from your home, first do a careful search of the house, thoroughly checking closets, piles of laundry, under beds, inside old refrigerators—wherever a child may crawl or hide. If you still cannot find your child, call your local law-enforcement agency *immediately*. Then call the National Center for Missing & Exploited Children at 1-800-THE-LOST. The search process must begin without delay. "When a child is abducted, the first few hours are absolutely critical in the recovery process," said John

Walsh, whose own son, Adam, was abducted from a Florida shopping mall and murdered. As host of Fox TV's *America's Most Wanted*, Walsh has captured dozens of criminals who have victimized innocent youngsters.

The Amber Alert: The Amber Alert is an immediate response system that utilizes the resources of the media to enlist the support of the public in finding children who have been kidnapped. This alert goes into effect immediately upon the issuing of an all-points police bulletin signaling the abduction of a child. Since the majority of youngsters who are murdered following their abductions are killed within 24 hours of being kidnapped, having the public's eyes and ears assisting during the critical early minutes and hours of a search is critical. The AMBER (*America's Missing: Broadcast Emergency Response*) Alert was created as a legacy to 9-year-old Amber Hagerman, who was kidnapped while riding her bicycle in Arlington, Texas. Following her abduction and murder, a public alert system was put into place by law-enforcement agencies and broadcasters to announce urgent bulletins regarding license plate numbers, vehicle information and descriptions of children involved in criminal child-abduction cases.

With time of the essence, radio and television stations interrupt their regularly scheduled programming to notify the public and to enlist their support in identifying certain individuals and specific vehicles. Radio stations repeat pertinent information and TV stations run a "crawl" on the bottom of the screen along with a picture of the child. Whenever possible, electronic highway billboards are used to display these bulletins. These signs instantly galvanize the driving community to be on the "look-out" and to assist in the search.

Code Adam: If your child is missing in a store, notify the store manager or security officer *immediately*. Ask to issue a Code Adam plan of action. Code Adam, one of the country's most powerful prevention programs, is now practiced in tens of thousands of retail stores across the country. The program is named in memory of Adam Walsh whose kidnapping in 1981 brought the crisis of missing children to national attention and led to the establishment of the National Center for Missing and Exploited Children.

Under a Code Adam plan, when a customer reports a missing child to a store employee, an alert is announced over the public-address system. A brief description of the child is broadcast and provided to all employees. Designated workers know to immediately stop their normal work and search for the child, as well as monitor all exits to help prevent the child from leaving the store. There is a full shut down of exits, as well as a search of all bathrooms and service areas.

If a child is not found within 10 minutes of initiating a storewide search, or if the child is seen accompanied by someone other than a parent or guardian, store personnel will contact the local police department and request assistance. At this time the child's name and identifying information will be entered into the National Crime Information Center (NCIC) Missing Person File and a national investigation will ensue.

INFANT ABDUCTION

A young mother sat in her room in a secure and well-managed private hospital in North Carolina feeding her newborn infant. A woman in a nurse's uniform came into the room and told the mother that she was taking the infant for tests and to have him weighed. The mother handed her infant over and, within minutes, the infant was out of the hospital, abducted by the woman impersonating a nurse. Happily, thanks to a speedy response by law enforcement and effective media coverage, the infant was recovered two days later, unharmed. When questioned, the abductor, convicted for kidnapping, simply said, "I wanted an infant for myself."

While not a widespread crime—perhaps a dozen cases or less per year throughout the country - the abduction of infants from hospitals and homes is, none-the-less, a grave concern for parents and expectant parents. The abduction of a newborn baby from a hospital nursery is a particularly heartbreaking crime with complex causes and baffling motivations.

As in the kidnapping of older children, the "typical"-type abduction may be carried out for objectives that are terrible, but generally comprehensible, such as revenge, profit, ransom, sexual gratification or power. The "nontraditional" taking of a baby, however, raises inexplicable motivations and reasons that are often not at all discernable. Some experts believe that an underlying motivation for the abduction of a newborn may be the need to "replace" an infant that the kidnapper has lost, or to provide a husband or boyfriend with the child that they believe he wants.

NCMEC has studied "typical" abductions from hospital nurseries and has developed a profile of kidnapper who is unknown to the new mother or the family and impersonates a nurse to gain access to the infant. Based on previous incidents, characteristics of a person who is most likely to commit such an act include the following:

- Female of "childbearing" age and often overweight.
- Most often relies on manipulation, lying, and deception.
- Frequently indicates that she has lost a baby or is incapable of having one.
- Has a husband or boyfriend who pressures her to have a child.
- Usually lives in the same community where the abduction takes place.
- Has visited various nursery and maternity units.
- Usually plans the abduction, but does not necessarily target a specific infant.
- Often becomes familiar with healthcare staff and victim parents.
- Provides "good" care to the baby once the abduction occurs.

New hospital security measures, live-scan technology and matching ID wrist and ankle bands for parents and babies maximize the safety and security of newborns. It is now, virtually impossible for security systems, cameras and alarms to fail to notice the kidnapping of an infant from a hospital. But, it is still necessary to require hospital ID from anyone who asks to take your baby to another location in the hospital as well question any person who does not belong on that floor. While in the hospital, mothers should never leave babies out of their direct line-of-sight. And, whenever possible, the infant's bassinet should be kept away from the doorway and the public hallway.

Once home with an infant, it is prudent not to add a street address to birth announcements printed in local papers. Similarly, outdoor decorations that announce an infant's arrival (such as pink or blue balloons tied to a mailbox) call unwarranted attention to the presence of the new infant in the home and are not recommended by security experts.

SEXUAL EXPLOITATION

The sexual exploitation of children is an unspeakable crime. And, the impact of this abuse is compounded when parents are silent to the mere existence of the problem. Society's unwillingness to address the horrific problem of sexual exploitation is a disservice to families and has a chilling effect upon all who could benefit from the solutions that open discussion of this problem could provide.

Children of all ages are vulnerable to sexual exploitation either by a family member, known assailant or unknown predator. Although recent high-profile cases in the news have involved young children, studies show that over 80 percent of targeted children are over the age of 12. Teenagers - and girls, in particular - are the most frequent victims of exploitation. Naturally, children are frightened, embarrassed and intimidated about revealing the exploitation that they may have experienced at the hands of a sexual predator. But parents cannot—and must not—join in that silence.

***Stranger Danger**:* In the HBO television special, "How to Raise a Street Smart Child," children provided their own descriptions of what a "stranger" might look like:

- *"A stranger sometimes wears a hat...sometimes a black or brown jacket and is a guy with a beard...some hair and a moustache and some glasses."*
- *"I think a stranger is like...a punk rocker [who] drinks beer all day and sits around in a vacant lot."*
- *"A stranger looks mean and ugly...a creep."*
- *"Mean. Hairy."*
- *"Bigger than you, bigger than most people."*

Interestingly, a child is far more likely to be sexually exploited by someone they already know and trust than a stranger lurking in the playground or waiting in a parking lot. The concept of "stranger danger" is an inaccurate notion, since most child molesters are not "strangers" to their victims. Even when an unknown individual initially befriends a child, within an hour of playing video games in an arcade or eating at a fast food restaurant, a formerly unknown individual will hardly seem like a stranger!

Being on the lookout for sexual deviants, monsters and dirty old men, therefore, will not safeguard your children. In fact, a focus on "strangers" can actually distract them from relying on their own judgment and sharpening the good instincts and inclinations they already have. According to Ernie Allen, President and CEO of NCMEC, "Stranger danger" is good information, but it's grossly incomplete. Children are at far greater risk with people they know, at least casually. It's not the guy who crawls out from under the bridge."

Sexual Predators: Those who victimize children come in every shape and size, age, gender ethnicity and walk of life. They rarely look like scary monsters and they are rarely even "strangers". Therefore, it is very important to help children focus on how this person actually behaves, rather than on how "suspicious" he may look. Personal safety for children has evolved from "Don't talk to strangers" to empowering youngsters to be skeptical and self-assured in all of their relationships.

Sexual predators are extremely shrewd. Unlike prevalent stereotypes, they are often well-mannered, affable individuals who will "court" a victim of interest with attention, compliments, and even gifts. Some of their approaches are so subtle that their victims may be unaware that they are even being lured. For example, certain deviant individuals will make sexual advances toward a child by touching them in a way that seems almost accidental or unintentional. Conveniently, some child molesters have a legitimate reason for touching a child—perhaps to hook a life jacket or fix a zipper—and this credible excuse for interaction acts as perfect "cover". Touching and other games of physical closeness, such as wrestling or the teaching of diving or ballet, are among those situations that scheming predators successfully "use" to fondle and entice children.

According to the American Psychological Association, "...there is no defense for child sexual abuse. It is always wrong." Child sexual exploitation can involve sexual molestation, online enticement of children for sexual acts, child prostitution, child sex tourism and even the possession of child pornography. Any type of sexual activity between children and adults is *unacceptable* because there is no such thing as a minor child being able to "consent" to sexual activity with an adult.

Not only is a sex between an adult and a child exploitative, it is also illegal. It is against the law for anyone to cause, induce, entice or coerce a child to engage in sexual conduct, or in the making of child pornography. Encouraging children to trust their own feelings and to act assertively when they sense that an advance is inappropriate will help them gain confidence in their own judgment. Since comfort is such a subjective feeling, giving children ownership of their decisions as well as their own sense of what is appropriate - and what is not - is very important. Children gain self-confidence when they know their parents will love and trust them - no matter what. Teaching children that they *always* have the right to say NO to unwelcome, uncomfortable attention is empowering.

Pedophiles: A pedophile is an adult who has recurrent sexual fantasies and urges about prepubescent children, usually youngsters under the age of *13*. These predators report a fascination with, and an intense sexual attraction to, young children of a particular age. Pedophiles often have had legitimate and long-term access to children, either as their coach, teacher or neighbor, counselor, etc.

Most pedophiles are considered either casual acquaintances or trusted older friends to their child victims. These individuals are rarely considered "strangers" and the children who are targeted are often unaware of their victimization. Typically, a pedophile seduces a child over a period of time, but that span can be quite short. For example, a man in his early 20's is in a video arcade, playing games next to an unsuspecting 11 year-old boy. The man begins to give the youngster tips and shortcuts to improve his game and then joins in the excitement when the child starts making winning points. He then passes him several quarters to continue playing and encourages his winning streak. After 10 minutes, the new, older "friend" suggests they go on to another arcade with even better games. The two leave laughing and excited about the video opportunities that await them. On the way to the second arcade, the man suggests that they stop at his apartment to pick up more money and to show the child his new video-game system. The boy willingly and happily goes into the man's apartment and they spend hours sitting next to each other on the couch playing video games. Using familiarity and friendship the man initiates a sexual encounter.

Because of the wide age disparity between adult pedophiles and their child victims, adult molesters of young children regularly use attractions like money, access to "cool" new people or even the authority of their uniforms, to entice their victims. They may take advantage of their professional stature to influence and lure youngsters and to gain their obedience and submission.

Pedophiles are masters of manipulation and sometimes use their devious abilities to gain the trust of children by offering favors, assistance and services to parents. Seduction is easily accomplished through "subtle" manipulation and persuasion. "Courting" activities like homework help, camping trips, movies and video arcade play give these individuals access to kids and credibility with them. Jobs like that of coach, teacher, bus driver, minister and camp counselor provide entrée to youngsters as well as the clout child molesters need to gain their victims' acquiescence.

Sometimes physical attention between the pedophile and his victim - tickling, wrestling or hugging - will take place in the presence of others. This brings particular legitimacy to the activity that will later be expanded in private. Children are often so impressed with the attention or privileges that they receive from an interested adult, they may worry that revealing the attention—or even the abusive activity—will cause the loss of these special privileges or gifts.

"I remember sitting around our kitchen table on the first night our son was taken," said Patty Wetterling, who began a foundation for children's safety following the 1989 abduction of her 11 year-year-old son. "When the investigators asked me, "Is there anybody who liked Jacob too much? Who gave him special attention or presents? Who wanted to take him places?" I never dreamed that a nice person could have taken our son or that the most common lure is attention and affection."

Social service agencies have found that many pedophiles strategically build relationships with single mothers in order to be in close physical proximity of their young children. Since many single parent situations involve domestic and financial problems and mothers working long hours outside of the home, these children are especially vulnerable to the attention of the pedophile. The "incestuous" or "interfamilial" molester is usually an adult male (often a stepfather or boyfriend of the mother) who lives with the child. The molestation is usually secretive and often conducted under verbal or physical threats and intimidation. The child-victims endure lifelong feelings of guilt, self-hatred and responsibility.

Pedophiles are typically married, adult males who live in the community and go to great lengths to conceal their sexual proclivities. Case histories analyzed by the Department of Justice reveal that these individuals often seek out publications and organizations that "normalize" their adult-child sexual practices. In addition, pedophiles are known to collect photographs of victims in sexually explicit positions and other child erotica and child-adult pornography.

Tragic and highly publicized child victimization cases have heightened society's awareness about pedophiles and also shattered some age-old myths. One of those myths is the "dirty old man" stereotype, depicting an old disheveled child- molester, unkempt and hunched over. In actuality, however, almost three quarters of convicted pedophiles are under the age of 35. The National Institute of Mental Health has reported that the typical sex offender begins molesting youngsters by the time he is 15.

Old stereotypes of pedophiles may also include the characteristic of mental retardation. Group homes for intellectually challenged people have not been welcomed in some communities, in part, because of old myths like the relationship between sexual deviancy and mental retardation. Not surprisingly, this stereotype is also not true with over 80% of convicted sex offenders testing within the normal range of intelligence.

PROTECTION

If there is a suspicion about an individual that needs to be addressed, children should feel confident that their parents would believe them—and believe *in* them. Empowering children to be strong and trust their own instincts is critical to reducing the possibility of their sexual exploitation. Developing a child's solid instincts and "street smarts" is key to their continuing safety.

Our society is obliged to protect its children. Therefore, safety from those who would harm kids in any way is the responsibility of all citizens. A first line of defense against pedophiles and abusers is the oversight and scrutiny of *all* individuals with whom your children have significant contact. This means checking the references of every babysitter, tutor, dentist, piano teacher and other adult that will be near your kids, particularly, those who may be alone with them.

Many states now maintain public databases and on-line registries that allow parents to cross check an individual's identity with current listings of convicted sex offenders. This distribution of information has occurred as a result of victims' rights legislation including the Jacob Wetterling Crimes Against Children and Sex Offender Registration Act. Recently, an expanded law supporting public notification of the home addresses of sex offenders was put into effect, prompted by the death of Megan Kanka in New Jersey. Seven-year-old Megan was lured into her neighbor's home with the promise of a puppy and brutally raped and murdered by a twice-convicted sex offender.

Parents can now access broad-based community notification services where information concerning their neighbors' criminal histories of sex offenses against children is available. According to law enforcement, stringent *sex* offender registration laws and related public information are effective because:

- As in the tragic case of Megan Kanka, convicted sex offenders pose a high risk of continuing their irrepressible urges and horrific behavior, even after they have received treatment and have been released from custody.
- The voting public agrees that public safety is more important than the "privacy" a convicted sex offender will lose by having the community aware of his identity and address.
- The release of certain information about individuals having a record of conviction for sexual crimes may be beneficial to the public, as well useful to the agencies that serve vulnerable children.

As necessary as keeping potential abductors away *from* children, is the need for ongoing prevention education *of* children. Children need skills for staying safe at all times—and from all situations that can lead to harm. Knowing how to avoid certain risks and staying levelheaded in the face of potential danger requires a commitment on the part of parents and schools to conscientiously train children. As children learn personal safety skills and protection strategies, they will gain self-confidence and independence.

Although the specific elements of prevention education vary, the goals of most of these programs encompass the following important objectives:

- Reduce the victimization of children
- Enhance the self-esteem of children
- Reduce guilt and blame associated with victimization

- Promote disclosure and discussion of abuse
- Coordinate community response teams
- Enhance communication within families
- Reinforce need for adult supervision and protection
- Discourage "offender behavior"

Numerous safety education programs are currently being implemented in schools throughout the country to introduce age-appropriate skills designed to reduce victimization. Because very young children and youngsters with special needs may be particularly vulnerable to victimization, it is of vital importance that school programs integrate an appropriate safety curriculum into each grade and special education program division. Classroom sessions should describe and reinforce the dangers of abuse and help kids to distinguish between those adult actions toward them that are appropriate and those that are not. Saying "No" to uncomfortable or unwanted overtures and telling a trusted adult if one should occur are important skills which can be taught—even to very young children.

Child-safety guides and curricula often include role-playing sequences that give children an opportunity to rehearse how to behave and what to say in a threatening situation. Opportunities to act out "What to do *if...*" are empowering exercises for youngsters and strengthen their resilience and confidence.

Similarly, working with law enforcement and safety specialists in school programs enable children to learn practical strategies for staying safe. For example, when children are asked how they might behave if an adult ever tried to grab them and pull them away, safety professionals say they should scream *words* (not just noises) such as…"This man is trying to take me" or "This person is not my father". Practicing these phrases permit children to "act out" how they might handle such an incident if one should ever occur.

Rehearsing responses to potential circumstances - from being lost in a shopping mall to using a code word if someone other than their parent must pick them up at school - creates a reserve of comfortable, learned behaviors. These interactive "what if" games can also be practiced at home where their practical and proven solutions can be reinforced.

HAS YOUR CHILD BEEN SEXUALLY EXPLOITED?

Children rarely lie about acts of sexual exploitation. Therefore, it is important that they are believed, praised and supported when - and if - they share their stories and secrets regarding abuse. Demonstrate your empathy and understanding should your child reveal traumatic or embarrassing details of a sexual experience. Parents must *be there* with love and support for their children and there is no room to be judgmental or critical at this time. Arrange appropriate medical and psychological support to help manage potential physical injuries or the psychological trauma of hurt, guilt and shame. It is also important to realize that many children will, initially, deny the experience of sexual exploitation to cover the anguish and humiliation.

Always emphasize that any abuse encountered was not their fault but the 100% responsibility of the adult abuser. Without overreacting or minimizing what has occurred, reinforce that "telling" was the right thing to do and that the child has done nothing wrong. It is important to inform law enforcement, child-protection services as well as your pediatrician who are expert in the legal, medical and psychological issues of child sexual victimization and the complex areas of diagnosis, evidence collection and treatment. At the same time, respect your child's right to privacy and do not discuss the incident with people who do not need to know.

As always, reassurance and communication are crucial to every age and stage of the parent-child relationship. It is important to have talks about difficult subjects, like sexual exploitation, regularly, and not save these subjects for times of crisis. Open communication and frank conversation should be an ongoing part of your family dynamic, so a structure is in place should a very serious concern, like that of possible exploitation, arise.

Since child-victims are often unwilling or simply unable to talk about abuse that has occurred, families must be alert to particular warning signs of exploitation and observe any of the following characteristics that a child might show:

- A compelling interest in spending time with a particular adult.
- The receipt of unexplained gifts, cell phone, video games or other expensive items.
- Increased interest in sexuality, questions about sex and interest in erotica and "mature" magazines.
- Specific, unexplained fears or an excessive fear of a certain place.
- Rashes, rawness and physical pain in private areas.

Instead of asking to explain some of these behaviors, outright, encourage your child to relay a story to facilitate sharing the details of traumatic incidents. For example, the neutral, "Tell me about this—," can promote discussion more easily than "Who gave you this and why?" Role-playing and drawing are also good techniques for telling stories, answering questions, expanding conversations and describing feelings. Within these safe discussions, parents can be a "witness" to experiences their child has endured and come into their circle of trust.

INTERNET

In the 1990's, our stereotype of a child molester was a man sitting on park bench stalking a potential victim in a neighborhood playground. In this setting, the identity of the predator was easy to discover and it was relatively simple to teach youngsters to *just say "No."* But, in this new millennium, the Internet has expanded our neighborhoods into a global electronic playground where personal park benches abound and multiple screen names, virtual pen palls, counterfeit photographs and instant identities have increased the complexities - and the risks - of predators reaching children. For many youngsters, learning how and when and to whom to just say "no" *to* is not so simple anymore.

In this new virtual playground, the man sitting on the park bench can convincingly pretend that he is the 12 -year-old girl who lives down the street. And, the highly technical and covert nature of on-line interaction exposes youngsters to content, ideas, images and individuals that may be totally inappropriate and unsafe. Children can now wander, unaccompanied, through all types of electronic neighborhoods and are increasingly vulnerable to crime and exploitation. Although there are many exciting and informative experiences awaiting children on the information superhighway, there are also many dangerous bumps and curves along the way.

Regardless of fears of on-line exposure and parental concerns for children's safety, the Internet is here to stay and is not going away anytime soon. Therefore, it seems prudent for parents to be cognizant of the serious risks that kids, today, face on the world-wide-web and help their families deal with these risks and challenges. These risks include:

***Solicitation*:** Perhaps the most feared and serious problem posed by the Internet is that of luring children *off* the Internet and into face-to-face meetings with Internet predators. These individuals are not "strangers" who break into houses and kidnap children; they are more subtle and manipulative predators who use on-line chat rooms, computer bulletin boards and e-mail exchanges to solicit victims.

Internet stalkers lure kids in with promises of video games, digital cameras, music- downloads, tickets to rock concerts and other "cool" products. Once they establish a favored relationship with an intended victim, they create a reason and opportunity to meet—preferably, without the knowledge of the child's parents. These predators are so clever that the young "victim" is usually unaware that she or he is even a victim, at all. On-line predators usually manipulate their target into being the party that instigates the meeting, thereby assuring that parents will not become involved.

The on-line predator is often 20+ years older than he reveals himself to be on the net and often cleverly researches personal information about his intended victim in chat rooms and on web sites. His familiarity with the victim's neighborhood and school make him seem more credible, trustworthy and younger to the youngsters on his e-mail or chat lists. The child on the receiving end of his e-mail or instant message is often an adolescent or teenaged girl who has embellished her own age and attributes as well. A face- to- face meeting with this individual is a risk not worth assuming.

Privacy: Disclosing identifying information - from a date of birth, to names of family members or hospital of birth - could inadvertently, put private information and access to it, into the hands of unscrupulous individuals. It is, therefore, crucial that children are alert to the need for limiting their personal information on-line that could jeopardize their own privacy and that of their family. This information gathering includes children's responses to seemingly innocent registrations for contests and sweepstakes and responding to polls and on-line surveys. Internet forgers and scam artists are adept at taking small bits of personal information and leveraging this data to get to other secure personal and financial data.

Sending photographs of children to public websites can also be a risky proposition. Never submit a picture of your child with any identifying information. That includes pictures taken in front of a street sign or in front of your home with the street number visible. Any information that links photos of children to their homes or schools compromises their safety.

E-Mail: Since Internet mail and other web- "spam" can be sent at little or no cost, just about everyone who has an e-mail address will receive bothersome advertisements and intrusive sexually explicit announcements at some time. This mail is recognized and deleted on most home computers but should be filtered out or removed before it becomes easily reached by children. Occasionally, familiar sounding return addresses are used as clever "come-ons" to entice children to open mail thereby capturing e-mail addresses linked to other information.

It is wise for both children and adults to avoid opening any mail from an unknown person or institution. Parents may also want to share an e-mail password with their youngsters and monitor and delete inappropriate e-mail and attachments before they reach a youngster. In order to avoid additional harassment, children should select e-mail addresses made up of words and numbers that do not reveal their names and are gender-neutral. This will not remedy the entire spam issue, but it will help.

Instant Messaging: IM has become as ubiquitous as the telephone for kids and teens in America, today. By simply typing a message to another Internet user signed-in on an IM service, a real-time conversation can take place. Instant messaging is an exciting vehicle with which children can communicate quickly, easily and anonymously. It also makes it simple to inadvertently reveal information that could place a child in harm's way.

Not surprisingly, sometimes the 14-year-old girl in the IM conversation turns out to be a forty-five year-old man. This illustrates the necessity for careful scrutiny of all on-line conversation partners, as IM users are often not whom they seem to be. Some instant messaging software can also be used for video chat where a camera attached to a computer can send personal photos and messages - in real time. And, IM conversations can also now take place via mobile phones where built in cameras can also make it possible to exchange text messages and photographs, instantaneously.

Chat Rooms: Chat rooms enable multiple participants to have their say during real-time conversations on a variety of discussion topics. Rooms are usually set up around shared interests, mutual experiences, fan clubs, etc. Live group conversations can take place among participants from across town or around the world and it is virtually impossible to control or secure an open chat. Chat rooms that welcome youngsters may also welcome adults who are looking to solicit children. These rooms are often closed to outsiders and unsupervised. While children sit within the safety of their own homes there may be adults, on-line, who will take advantage of a child's level of comfort and trust in that setting.

Pornography: In the virtual world of the Internet, pornography takes on new and insidious roles. Technology has made the distribution of X-rated photographs widespread and the creation of "virtual kiddie porn", all too simple. Just coming across a pornographic website can shock and abuse a child as well as provide unsolicited links to other adult sites. Some pornographic sites are designed to entice children through innocent spelling mistakes in order to expose them to specific advertising and graphic sexual images. Slight name differences or the distinction between .com and .net are used as "come-ons" to sexually explicit material. Pornography can be so easily accessed that it seems particularly unfair to promote the material to very young children who have made no effort to even look for it.

In addition to exposure to sexually explicit material on the web, the use of children *in* pornography has devastating and long lasting effects. Victims range from those youngsters who have seen "kiddie porn" to those who are seen in it. Being photographed during sexual abuse intensifies the child's feelings of shame and disgrace. And, these children face a continuing stigma if the images are seen on the Internet. Images on the world-wide-web can be downloaded by people everywhere where in the world and will remain in cyberspace, indefinitely. Unfortunately, children can unknowingly participate in virtual porn, as photographs of children's faces are regularly superimposed onto nude bodies of others and widely distributed on the word wide web.

PREVENTION

Obviously, certain net-based content and images are not appropriate for children. There is an enormous amount of adult content on-line which is, unequivocally, not suitable for youngsters. The Internet, called a "public park" for all, however, cannot censor or discriminate what flows through it. Nor, can it monitor the intensity, adult nature, truth and accuracy, explicit sexuality or blatant violence of the material.

Parental Supervision: It is the responsibility of parents to carefully monitor their children's computer use, maximizing the Internet's remarkable potential for youngsters and minimizing the obvious risks of being on-line. Safeguarding children from dangerous situations requires close and constant oversight. There is no substitute for intensive supervision of children on-line in order to become "street smart" and savvy users of the Internet.

It may be an understatement to suggest that there is some content on the Internet that is so inappropriate that it is dangerous for children to even stumble upon it for an instant. There is certainly revolting and unfathomable material lurking in every dark corner of the world-wide-web; hate sites, sites that give instructions about how to build bombs, forums to discuss ways to commit suicide, sites that encourage the use of drugs and even sites promising access to terrorist materials.

Rating systems and filters: Blocking and filtering software can limit children's ability to access much of the inappropriate content on the Internet. Ratings, filtering systems and blocking devices are available to help parents supervise selections and curb access to unsuitable content and images. Although these programs can minimize the risks, they are, by no means, foolproof mechanisms for keeping children safe on the net.

Rating systems, such as the Electronic Software Ratings Board's (ESRB)'s "Kid", "Teen" and "Mature" video game ratings, provide useful information for families and help them to more precisely guide their children's selection of on-line games and interactive websites. Most filters, however, rely on web-site operators to "rate" their own sites, voluntarily, and very few do. Internet browsers can be configured to only allow visits to websites rated at a specified level. However, this is not foolproof and many unrated sites with appropriate content will be filtered out as well.

Some blocking devises enable parents to monitor and exclude certain words and phrases from a child's incoming e-mail as well as from certain websites. These world exclusion software programs are verbal filters that can be made sensitive to some hate speech, violent threats, overtly racist and sexual remarks, specific curse words and vulgarity. However, the systems that limit certain words may be unable prevent instant messages or other pornographic material from coming through and even "popping up", unexpectedly, on your child's computer screen. And remember, while the word SEX may be blocked, S-X will not.

Clearly, there is no electronic mechanism or software program that can substitute for parental supervision. As the children's on-line world extends to chat rooms, newsgroups, Internet music and video services, cell phones, video-game consoles and built-in camera phones, parents must be vigilant about watching over children as they drive the information super-highway.

Reporting: If your child receives a sexually explicit e-mail message, pornographic image or is approached on-line by someone who wants to arrange an in-person meeting, you should report this activity to the National Center for Missing and Exploited Children's *CyberTipline* at 1-800-THE-LOST. Operated by NCMEC in partnership with the Federal Bureau of Investigation, Bureau of Customs Immigration Enforcement, U.S. Secret Service, U.S. Postal Inspection Service and state and local Crimes Against Children Task Forces, the *CyberTipline* is a national clearinghouse for reporting Internet abuses and solicitation crimes against children. These crimes include:

- Creation of child pornography or depiction of a child under the age of 18, engaged in sexually explicit conduct
- Use of the Internet to entice, invite, or persuade a child to meet for sexual acts, or to help arrange such a meeting
- Child prostitution
- Unsolicited obscene material with attached images or hyperlinks sent to a child under the age of 16

The National Center for Missing and Exploited Children has developed some helpful safety tips. These tips are also available on the NCMEC website (www. missing kids.com).

General safety tips for young children

I KNOW MY NAME, ADDRESS, TELEPHONE NUMBER, AND MY PARENTS' NAMES.

I ALWAYS CHECK FIRST WITH MY PARENTS OR THE PERSON IN CHARGE BEFORE I GO ANYWHERE OR GET INTO A CAR, EVEN WITH SOMEONE I KNOW.

I ALWAYS CHECK FIRST WITH MY PARENTS BEFORE I ACCEPT ANYTHING FROM ANYONE.

I ALWAYS TAKE A FRIEND WITH ME WHEN I GO PLACES OR PLAY OUTSIDE.

I SAY NO IF SOMEONE TRIES TO TOUCH ME IN A WAY THAT MAKES ME FEEL SCARED OR UNCOMFORTABLE.

IT'S OK TO SAY NO, AND I KNOW THAT THERE WILL ALWAYS BE SOMEONE WHO CAN HELP ME.

I KNOW THAT I CAN TELL MY PARENTS OR A TRUSTED ADULT IF I FEEL SCARED, UNCOMFORTABLE, OR CONFUSED.

I AM STRONG, SMART, AND HAVE THE RIGHT TO BE SAFE.

Safety tips for going to school

ALWAYS TAKE A FRIEND WHEN WALKING OR RIDING YOUR BIKE TO AND FROM SCHOOL.

STAY WITH A GROUP WHILE WAITING AT THE BUS STOP. IT'S SAFER AND MORE FUN TO BE WITH YOUR FRIENDS.

IF ANYONE BOTHERS YOU WHILE GOING TO OR FROM SCHOOL, GET AWAY FROM THAT PERSON, AND TELL A TRUSTED ADULT LIKE YOUR PARENTS OR TEACHER.

IF SOMEONE YOU DON'T KNOW OR FEEL COMFORTABLE WITH OFFERS YOU A RIDE, SAY NO.

IF SOMEONE FOLLOWS YOU, GET AWAY FROM HIM OR HER AS QUICKLY AS YOU CAN. ALWAYS BE SURE TO TELL YOUR PARENTS OR A TRUSTED ADULT WHAT HAPPENED.

TRUST YOUR FEELINGS. IF SOMEONE MAKES YOU FEEL SCARED OR UNCOMFORTABLE, GET AWAY AS FAST AS YOU CAN AND TELL A TRUSTED ADULT.

General safety tips for teens

DON'T GO OUT ALONE. THERE IS SAFETY IN NUMBERS. THIS RULE ISN'T JUST FOR LITTLE KIDS; IT APPLIES TO TEENS, TOO.

ALWAYS TELL AN ADULT WHERE YOU'RE GOING. LETTING SOMEONE KNOW WHERE YOU'LL BE AT ALL TIMES IS SMART.

SAY NO IF SOMEONE TOUCHES YOU IN A WAY THAT MAKES YOU FEEL UNCOMFORTABLE.

WHETHER IT IS PRESSURE ABOUT SEX, DRUGS, OR SOMETHING THAT YOU KNOW IS WRONG, BE STRONG AND STAND YOUR GROUND.

WHEN HOME ALONE…

CHECK OUT THE HOUSE BEFORE ENTERING. GO TO A SAFE PLACE TO CALL FOR HELP IF SOMETHING DOESN'T SEEM RIGHT.

LOCK THE DOOR. CALL YOUR MOM OR DAD WHEN YOU GET HOME TO LET THEM KNOW YOU'RE SAFE.

NEVER TELL CALLERS YOUR PARENTS AREN'T HOME. INSTEAD SAY THEY CAN'T COME TO THE PHONE.

DON'T OPEN THE DOOR TO ANYONE WHO COMES TO YOUR HOME UNLESS IT'S A FRIEND OR RELATIVE.

Tips for Internet safety

I WILL NOT GIVE OUT PERSONAL INFORMATION SUCH AS MY ADDRESS, TELEPHONE NUMBER OR THE NAME AND LOCATION OF MY SCHOOL WITHOUT PERMISSION.

I WILL TELL MY PARENTS IF I COME ACROSS INFORMATION THAT MAKES ME FEEL UNCOMFORTABLE.

I WILL NEVER AGREE TO GET TOGETHER WITH SOMEONE I "MEET" ON LINE WITHOUT FIRST CHECKING WITH MY PARENTS.

I WILL NEVER SEND A PERSON MY PICTURE OR ANYTHING ELSE.

I WILL NOT RESPOND TO ANY MESSAGES THAT ARE MEANT TO MAKE ME FEEL UNCOMFORTABLE.

I WILL TALK WITH MY PARENTS SO THAT WE CAN SET UP RULES FOR GOING ON LINE.

I WILL PRACTICE GOOD "NETIQUETTE" AND NOT DO ANYTHING THAT HURTS OTHER PEOPLE.

General child-safety tips for parents

PARENTS SHOULD TAKE AN ACTIVE ROLE IN THEIR CHILDREN'S LIVES. PARENTS SHOULD KNOW WHERE THEIR CHILDREN ARE AT ALL TIMES, AND BE FAMILIAR WITH THEIR CHILDREN'S FRIENDS AND DAILY ACTIVITIES. PARENTS SHOULD TEACH CHILDREN TO ASK FOR PERMISSION BEFORE GOING WITH ANYONE. PARENTS SHOULD CHILDREN THAT THEY SHOULD ALWAYS TELL THEIR PARENTS ABOUT WHAT HAPPENED. PARENTS SHOULD ASSURE THEIR CHILDREN THEY ALWAYS HAVE THE RIGHT TO SAY "NO". CHILDREN SHOULD KNOW THEIR ADDRESS AND TELEPHONE NUMBER, AND HOW TO CONTACT PARENTS PARENTS SHOULD DEVICE A CODE WORD THAT THE CHILD CAN LEARN IN CASE THERE IS AN EMERGENCY. PARENTS SHOULD TEACH THEIR CHILDREN HOW TO DIAL "911" TO ASK FOR HELP IN AN EMERGENCY.

ON-LINE HEALTH AND SAFETY RESOURCES FOR FEARLESS PARENTS

About Our Kids www.aboutourkids.org

Administration for Children and Families www.acf.dhhs.gov

American Academy of Addiction Psychiatry www.aaap.org

American Academy of Child and Adolescent Psychiatry www.aacap.org

American Academy of Pediatrics www.aap.org

American Counseling Association www.counseling.org

American Foundation for Suicide Prevention www.afsp.org

American Medical Association www.ama-assn.org

American Psychiatric Association www.psych.org

American Psychoanalytic Association www.apsa.org

American Psychological Association www.apa.org

American Red Cross www.redcross.org

American School Counselors Association www.schoolcounselor.org

American Society of Adolescent Psychiatry www.adolpsych.org

America's Health Together www.healthtogether.org

Anxiety Disorders Association of America www.adaa.org

Autism Society of America www.autism-society.org

Association of Schools of Public Health www.asph.org

Boys and Girls Clubs of America www.bgca.org

Centers for Disease Control and Prevention www.cdc.gov

Center for Health and Health Care in Schools www.healthinschools.org

Center for Mental Health Services www.mentalhealth.org

Center for the Study and Prevention of Violence www.colorado.edu/cspv

Child Advocate www.childadvocate.net

Child and Family Web Guide www.cfw.tufts.edu/index.html

Childhelp USA www.childhelpusa.org

Children with Disabilities www.childrenwithdisabilities.ncjrs.org

Children's Health Council www.chconline.org

Child Welfare League of America www.cwla.org

Child Safety on the Information Highway www.safekids.com

Children and Adults with Attention Deficit Disorder www.chadd.org

Committee for Children www.cfchildren.org

Connect for Kids www.connectforkids.org

Court Appointed Special Advocates www.nationalcasa.org

The Cross Cultural Health Care Program www.xculture.org

Department of Health and Human Services Administration for Children and Families www.acf.dhhs.gov

Department of Justice, Office for Domestic Preparedness www.ojp.usdoj.gov/odp

Facts for Health www.factsforhealth.org

Families for Depression Awareness www.familyaware.org

Federation of Families for Children's Mental Health www.ffcmh.org

Federal Emergency Management Agency www.fema.gov

Freedom From Fear www.freedomfromfear.org

Harvard Medical Library www.med.harvard.edu

Healthfinder www.healthfinder.gov

Healthfinder Español www.healthfinder.gov/espanol

Injury Prevention Web www.injurypreventionweb.org

International Association for Child and Adolescent Psychiatry and Allied Professions www.iacapap.org

Keep Schools Safe www.keepschoolssafe.org

Mental Health Liaison Group www.mhlg.org

National Alliance for the Mentally Ill www.nami.org

National Advisory Committee on Children and Terrorism www.bt.cdc.gov/children

National Association of County and City Health Officials www.naccho.org

National Association of Attorneys General and National School Boards Association www.keepschoolssafe.org

National Association of School Psychologists www.nasponline.org

National Black Child Development Institute www.nbcdi.org

National Center for Children Exposed to Violence www.nccev.org

National Center for Juvenile Justice and Mental Health www.ncmhjj.com

National Center for Learning Disabilities www.ld.org

National Center for Missing and Exploited Children www.missingkids.org

National Center for Post Traumatic Stress Disorder www.ncptsd.org

National Child Registry www.childreg.com

National Foundation for Abused and Neglected Children www.gangfreekids.org

National Institute of Health www.nih.gov

National Institute of Mental Health www.nimh.nih.gov

National Institute on Drug Abuse www.nida.nih.gov

National Mental Health Association www.nmha.org

National Parent Information Network www.npin.org

National School Safety Center www.nssc1.org

Office of Homeland Security www.whitehouse.gov/homeland

Office of Juvenile Justice and Delinquency Prevention www.ojjdp.ncjrs.org

PBS Kids www.pbs.org/kids

Prevent Child Abuse America www.preventchildabuse.org

Report of the Surgeon General's Conference on Children's Mental Health www.surgeongeneral.gov/topics/cmh/childreport.htm

Safe and Drug Free Schools Program www.ed.gov/offices/OESE/SDFS

Safe Schools Coalition www.ed.mtu.edu/safe/

Safer Child www.saferchild.org

Stand For Children www.stand.org

Substance Abuse and Mental Health Services Administration www.samhsa.gov

U.S. Department of Health and Human Services www.hhs.gov

World Health Organization www.who.ch

Zero to Three www.zerotothree.org

ABOUT THE AUTHOR

A distinguished psychologist and nationally known authority on child development, victimization and trauma and loss, Dr. Boehm is a trusted parenting resource and frequent guest on television. A longtime advocate for responsible children's media, she headed Public Responsibility and Standards at MTV Networks/Nickelodeon and was Vice President of the Fox Children's Network. She has given testimony before Congress, served as Director of Children's Advertising Review for the Council of Better Business Bureaus and as a faculty member at the City University of New York. Dr. Boehm has written for Child, Parenting, Psychology Today, Working Mother, Redbook and Exceptional Parent magazines and is the author of the new trade paperback, The 2004 Official Guide to the Right Toys. She received her undergraduate degree from Boston University and her masters and doctorate from Columbia University. The mother of two, she divides her time between New York City and the Berkshires.

Printed in the United States
16333LVS00007B/1-102